HUMANITARIAN
JESUS

CHRISTIAN BUCKLEY
& RYAN DOBSON

HUMANITARIAN
JESUS

SOCIAL
JUSTICE
AND THE
CROSS

MOODY PUBLISHERS
CHICAGO

Scripture taken from The Holy Bible, English Standard Version. Copyright © 2000; 2001 by Crossway Bibles, a division of Good News Publishers. Used by permission. All rights reserved.

All websites listed herein are accurate at the time of publication, but may change in the future or cease to exist. The listing of website references and resources does not imply publisher endorsement of the site's entire contents. Groups, corporations, and organizations are listed for informational purposes, and listing does not imply publisher endorsement of their activities.

Editor: Christopher Reese
Interior Design: Smartt Guys design
Cover Design: Brand Navigation, LLC
Photo Credit for Christian Buckley: Aaron Chang

Library of Congress Cataloging-in-Publication Data

Buckley, Christian.
    Humanitarian Jesus : social justice and the cross / Christian Buckley, Ryan Dobson.
       p. cm.
    Includes bibliographical references.
    ISBN 978-0-8024-5263-4
    1. Social justice—Religious aspects—Christianity. 2. Christianity and justice. 3. Church and social problems. I. Dobson, Ryan. II. Title.
    BR115.J8B83 2010
    261.8--dc22

                                                                    2010000385

This book is printed on acid free recycled paper containing 30% PCW (Post Consumer Waste) and manufactured in the United States of America by Bethany Press.

We hope you enjoy this book from Moody Publishers. Our goal is to provide high-quality, thought-provoking books and products that connect truth to your real needs and challenges. For more information on other books and products written and produced from a biblical perspective, go to www.moodypublishers.com or write to:

Moody Publishers
820 N. LaSalle Boulevard
Chicago, IL 60610

1 3 5 7 9 10 8 6 4 2

Printed in the United States of America

This book is dedicated to our fathers,
who have taught us well to seek the Lord and do right in His eyes
2 Chronicles 26:4–5

CONTENTS

"I'm always worried about being satisfied. When you become satisfied, you sort of like, you just die."

—JACK WHITE

PREFACE

Getting involved in a book project like this, for me, is kind of like dropping into a big wave. On one hand it's very exciting, and on the other it's extremely scary. I'm so fortunate to work with Christian on this project. I have faith and confidence that when I attach my name with his I'll be the better for it. Whenever you write, or speak, or create something, there is a desired outcome for the audience. And, as the author or creator, the responsibility is up to you for that outcome. There is a huge responsibility involved. Someone is going to pay hard-earned money to read something you were so passionate about that you took the time to put thought to paper, seek out a like-minded publisher, submit your creation to editors to criticize, and then offer it to the general public. You can't let them down. It's very personal and intimate, while being publicly consumed.

This book is the product of passion. It's out of our love for people and Christ that we embarked on this adventure of writing. Because of my history with Christian, I kind of jumped into this without much forethought, but as the process unfolded, it became deeper. You can't just unlearn, you can't ignore, you can't deny. And because of that it either changes you or it splits you. This book has done that for me, and that is my hope for you, the reader. Think deeply. Ponder the thoughts and passions of the writers and interviewees. Open your eyes to the humanity surrounding you. Some of it is beautiful, joyous, exuberant, and satisfied, and some of it is broken, bleeding, hungry, cold, and alone. Keep your eyes and hearts open as you read, and keep asking yourself, "What *could* I do?" If we keep ourselves from becoming complacent, what kind of a change can we make?

Thank you for reading this book.

God bless you,
Ryan Dobson

You cannot find a man anywhere, however uncivilised or wild, who is without some idea of religion. This is because we have all been created to know the majesty of our Creator and, in knowing it, to think more highly of it than anything else. . . .

Now, eternal and immortal life can be found nowhere except in God. It follows, then, that the main care and concern of our life should be to seek God. We should long for him with all the affection of our hearts, and not find rest and peace anywhere except in him alone.

—JOHN CALVIN, 1536[1]

INTRODUCTION

Humanitarian: *A person devoted to promoting the welfare of humanity.*[2]
Jesus: *The human-divine Son of God; the great High Priest who intercedes for His people at the right hand of God; the central figure of human history; the one who conquered sin and death; and the way, truth and life through whom alone can we be reconciled with God.*[3]

This world is broken. Make no mistake: no matter how your life has unfolded, God intended it to be different. In the beginning, when God created, all was good. It worked. But we broke it. We took pure Good and exchanged it for something impure and broken. We exchanged the truth that God created us to live with Him for the lie that there was something better. We exchanged what did matter for what didn't matter. We exchanged the magnificence of His eternal perspective for the banality of our temporal one. And we continue to do it today.

So we live in a broken world, groaning under the weight of its decay, haunted by the knowledge that it could have been different. We see shadows

13

and remnants of the perfection that was and is to be, but live in, with, and through the vestiges of brokenness.

We don't have to look very hard or dig very deep to discover the inescapable tragedy that surrounds us. Children starve, human beings are sold, multitudes die of malaria, and millions live in the streets. Medical epidemics sweep over countries like consuming wildfires, even while solutions exist. Devastating hunger plagues some homes, while culinary abundance exists in others—suffocating poverty living next to untold riches. In the midst of all of this, we grasp for meaning, hope, direction, and love, but often don't find them. We intuitively know that the world should be different.

This is the world Jesus confronted. He created this world and then became a part of it. Imagine what it must have felt like for Him to walk in what had been *good*, but was then corrupt and fallen. The God of the universe, the Creator of light and Giver of life, found Himself surrounded by injustice, sickness, hunger, and depravity.

If ever there existed a man for a job, it was Christ to fix the plight of His creation. It was Christ to restore the order of His Kingdom. Surely there has never been another human with proficiencies so perfectly fit to conquer the issues of global poverty, hunger, sickness, injustice, and oppression. It is odd then that of all the titles given to Christ, "humanitarian" has not been one of them.

In reality, there has never existed a person who taught and lived more for the welfare of humanity. Christ was a humanitarian for sure, but not the kind you would expect. He healed many, when He had the power to heal all. He fed many, when He had the power to feed all. He restored a few to life, liberated a few from suffering, and redressed a few injustices. But in all these matters, His work was totally incomplete from a statistical perspective. In fact, of all His work and effort, He actually focused on just one ultimate task. It was the task He prayed three times to have pass from Him, and after which He declared it finished.

Christ healed, He fed, He touched, and He loved; but above all, He conquered death and sin to provide an eternal solution to brokenness and separation.

So here we stand at the beginning of the twenty-first century, being called to action—to get out there and touch a life, meet a need, and do what Jesus did. Without question we should respond to this call; there has never been a greater time or opportunity for Christians to get out of the church and into the world. Every Christian is called by Christ to radically invest in His creation, to walk as He walked, and to serve Him so that His purposes can continue to be fulfilled on earth. Jesus made immense social investment while on earth. But that is only part of the story.

We hold the power to do good on an unprecedented scale—and we should. But we should also ask ourselves *why*? Why should we invest in the suffering of all creation? Why did Jesus invest and why didn't He finish the task? Is there really a conflict between evangelism and social justice or just in the ways we understand them? These are the questions this book seeks to answer. But before we engage them, a few notes are in order.

Without question the issues discussed in this book are not easily resolved. This is due in part to the fact that there is no single, universally accepted approach to reconciling our spiritual nature and destiny with physical death, sorrow, and tragedy. There has rarely been agreement among modern Christians on how the work of evangelism and the work of social justice can be accomplished in harmony. One of the patriarchs of the social gospel, Walter Rauschenbusch, when attempting to set down a complete understanding of the topic, admitted that his effort was both momentous and perhaps audacious.[4]

The topic of social justice, social Christianity, the social gospel, or the role of temporal humanitarian investment by Christians is expansive and any discussion must take place within clear boundaries to avoid confusion and frustration. At the outset, we must state that the foundation for our writing and thinking on this subject is the Bible, because we believe that it is the truth—the inerrant, authoritative, and final Word of God.

Second, this book is focused on the question of social investment and humanitarian effort as it relates to individuals, and in particular such work that is done by Christians for those who are not Christians. Of course, Christians have the responsibility to care for our brothers and sisters in Christ who are suffering around the globe under the identical situations discussed in these chapters (James 2:15–17; 1 John 3:16–18), and we are most assuredly lacking in our collective efforts. That said, this book does not cover that topic.

This also means that we will not specifically be addressing the need for corporate or societal efforts by the church (in the sense of local congregations of believers) or institutions. The present work is dedicated to how the individual follower of Christ should consider and react to these issues.

Third, this is not an academic treatment of these topics. We hope it is well reasoned and well supported, but it is neither scholarly in nature nor written from the perspective of a particular academic discipline (e.g., sociology, political science, economics, etc.). Detailed analyses of the historical social gospel have been written by competent scholars, and we have referenced many of these in our endnotes. If anything, this work has been written as an argument, intended to provoke consideration and reaction.[5]

Fourth, the interviews and quotations in this book are not necessarily included because we agree with them entirely, but rather because we think they are worthy of consideration. Conversely, the interviewees in part two of this book, and the organizations they represent, may not agree with everything we have written. While part one of the book was substantially written before we did any of the interviews, the interviewees did not review the book before granting us interviews and therefore are not accountable for our opinions and conclusions.

Finally, it is our intent to challenge you to think through these issues deeply and carefully. In the first part of this work we are asking you to reconsider your view of humanitarian efforts. In the second part, we are asking you to exercise your renewed or solidified thinking by engaging interviewees and ideas you may be encountering for the first time. Both Ryan and I (Christian) are passionate about this topic, and while I have done the writing, we have engaged this work together in the hope that wherever you stand now, this book will move you closer toward Christ's call in your life.

PART ONE:

In Search of the
HUMANITARIAN
JESUS

The things that are seen are transient,

but the things that are unseen are eternal.

—2 CORINTHIANS 4:18

Chapter 1

IS DOING GOOD, GOOD ENOUGH?

Buckled to the ground, covered in dirt, aching from a life of sickness and desperation; frantic for healing from a disease you don't understand, but know has killed your children, killed your family, killed your people, and is killing you.

~~~

Thirsty to your core, sun pounding down, willing to give all you have for a solitary drop of clean water. Praying that a well can be dug, water can be found, life can go on.

~~~

It's just another cold night on the concrete, getting harder by the day, but there's nowhere to go. The rain starts to fall and the wind picks up, but there's nowhere to go. You beg for food, for money, for hope.

~~~

Legs raw with welts from infected mosquitoes. You can hear your baby scream and know she is dying but are helpless to change her malaria-induced destiny. You desperately swat and brush the bugs away, but you know your other children will be bitten too.

You're still lying on the ground, covered in dirt, desperate for healing. Another year goes by; still no clean water, still no hope for life. Two more children gone, your welt-scarred legs a constant reminder of their fate . . .

Your life is draining out and deliverance doesn't come. You cling to the last bit, grip it in your fingers, because you fear the end and what waits beyond your last breath. You know there is something greater, but you don't know what. You pray that God, if there is a God, will reach out and speak. You pray for an answer to forever, but it doesn't come. Just one more shot, one more pill, one more glass of dirty water, one more lonely, hungry night, and then it is all over. You reach your last breath and then eternity.

Some two thousand years ago, while leaving a town filled with broken, hurting, hungry people, Jesus paused along the road to Jerusalem in response to a cry for mercy from Bartimaeus, a blind beggar. Jesus engaged him with a question: "What do you want me to do for you?" Bartimaeus responded with a request for sight, which Christ granted.[1]

On the surface, the encounter seems ordinary—a reasonable question with an obvious answer. But Bartimaeus was poor and blind; his life was unmistakably marked by his affliction, and Christ knew that before the encounter ever occurred. So why did He ask the question?

Bartimaeus lived with the seen and the unseen—the transient and the eternal. But for Christ, everything was seen—everything was eternal. Christ understood the reality that we see with physical eyes, the visible consequences of a broken world in our lives, but we often fail to see with spiritual eyes the eternal consequences that go with them. Christ said to people, "Your sins are forgiven," and they responded, "Yes, Lord, but I can't see." He said, "Your sins are forgiven," and they said, "Yes, Lord, but I'm hungry." "Your sins are forgiven . . ." "Yes, Lord, but I'm dying."

Today around our world, people just like Bartimaeus have real physical needs. But like you and me, they also have spiritual needs. Each of us, whether we realize it or not, needs to see Christ for who He really is. We need to have a powerful encounter with our Creator that can transform our eternal destinies, not just our physical circumstances.

PHYSICAL AND SPIRITUAL NEEDS

In 1854, Charles Spurgeon began preaching in London. The city was engulfed in such poverty and social injustice that just a decade later, another London minister, William Booth, left his pulpit and walked out into the streets, founding what would become the Salvation Army to reach the poor, homeless, hungry, and destitute. It was in this London that on June 18, 1876, Spurgeon preached the following words:

> Men have enough practical sense always to judge that if professed Christians do not care for their bodily wants, there cannot be much sincerity in their zeal for men's souls. If a man will give me spiritual bread in the form of a tract, but would not give me a piece of bread for my body, how can I think much of him? Let practical help to the poor go with the spiritual help which you render to them. If you would help to keep a brother's soul alive in the higher sense, be not backward to do it in the more ordinary way.[2]

Perhaps from these words, Spurgeon was believed to have said, "If you want to give a hungry man a tract, then wrap it up in a sandwich." Many since that time have struggled with this idea and have reflected that it might be better said that if you want to give a hungry man a sandwich, you should wrap it up in a tract.

The sandwich-and-tract debate highlights the basic reality of Christ's encounter with each of us. The hungry need food, but we all need redemption. The blind need sight, but we all need to see our condition and separation from God. Every encounter between God and us has these two dimensions—the physical and the spiritual.

Christ came to seek and to save the lost. He moved through the world reaching out in perfect love to bring people to Himself and His offer of eternal life. The focus of Christ's life, as given by His father, was to provide a singular opportunity for whosoever might believe in Him to not perish but have everlasting, reconciled life with Him. This fact is the cornerstone of Scripture.

Yet on His way to the cross, Christ invested His life in people. Not just twelve people, but countless thousands of men, women, and children. He fed, healed, and raised them from the dead. He demonstrated the purest form of selfless love the world has ever seen. And incredibly, He did this for both those who would come to follow Him and those who would not.

Even though He knew that the world was passing away and that all of the temporal afflictions He encountered would pass away with it, He provided temporal solutions for thousands of people who primarily had an eternal, spiritual need. Stated simply, Christ "did good" and instructed us to do the same.

Christ's attention to both spiritual and physical needs is illustrated for us frequently in the Gospels, but with no greater simplicity than in Mark 1:32–39, where after healing Simon's mother-in-law and teaching in the synagogue in Capernaum, word of His power and authority began to spread through Galilee, attracting the masses:

> That evening at sundown they brought to him all who were sick or oppressed by demons. And the whole city was gathered together at the door. And he healed many who were sick with various diseases, and cast out many demons. . . .
>
> And rising very early in the morning, while it was still dark, he departed and went out to a desolate place, and there he prayed. And Simon and those who were with him searched for him, and they found him and said to him, "Everyone is looking for you." And he said to them, "Let us go on to the next towns, that I may preach there also, for that is why I came out." And he went throughout all Galilee, preaching in their synagogues and casting out demons.

Because of Christ's compassion and healing ministry, the entire city gathered at His door and brought Him *all* who were sick and oppressed, but He healed and delivered only *many* of them. When they returned the next morning looking for Him to finish His work, He was gone to spend time with His Father. When they finally found Him, instead of healing and delivering the remaining sick and oppressed who needed His touch, He left the town to go elsewhere to preach because that is why He came.

Christ didn't minimize His compassionate work of healing and delivering the oppressed, but He also made clear that He came to *preach*, to proclaim a message as a herald with authority and gravity such that people would listen to and obey His words.[3] Christ did both things with clarity, harmony, and purpose.

AN EMERGING OPPORTUNITY

For perhaps the first time in human history the question of "can" in relation to humanitarian and social investment has been rendered largely irrelevant. Modern technologies in the areas of travel, communication, science, and medicine have provided mankind with an amazing capacity to identify global need and respond in ways that were unattainable even fifty years ago. Science and technology have given mankind the practical capacity to "do good" on an unprecedented scale.

In 1907, Walter Rauschenbusch, in his incendiary work *Christianity and the Social Crisis,* opined that "the world is getting small."[4] We can now say with confidence that he was right. Consider that in 1950, widespread international air travel was yet to be developed. In 1960, consumer debt was just emerging as an idea, let alone a tool for personal commerce and global influence. In 1975, most American families had no computer in their home. In 1990, most American families had never used a cell phone. In 1994, most American families had never used the Internet.

In just fifty years, the landscapes of information, communication, consumer debt, and travel have changed forever. If you wanted, you could find a village in Africa today, board an airplane tomorrow, and within a few days be sending photos, emails, and telephone calls home about the needs you are encountering. Even fifteen years ago, this would have been difficult, if not impossible.

Closer to home, we can make donations with the click of a mouse, provide shoes for children by shopping online, support AIDS relief by buying a T-shirt, and raise awareness of almost anything by wearing the right colored rubber wristband or lapel pin.

Individuals like Bill Clinton, Warren Buffett, Bill Gates, Bono, Oprah Winfrey, Caroline Kennedy, and others are leading a growing number of influential men and women in a discussion about giving, charitable investment, and social entrepreneurship. There can be no question that, at least in part, the latter half of the first decade of the twenty-first century is marked by an emphasis on our individual and collective need to "do good."

The political and social dialogue concerning religion is largely refocusing on the idea that we can be united in love, compassion, and the betterment of mankind. Not surprisingly, the Christian church is experiencing a resurgence of the social gospel with congregations, leaders, individuals, and nonprofit groups seeking to make significant social investments in their communities and around the world. "Doing good" is a new commodity within the corporate and philanthropic worlds. But for the Christian, the concept is more complex.

Now, more than ever, because of the almost limitless possibilities for global interaction and social investment, we need to start asking, "Of all the good that can be done in the world, what good *should* be done and *why*?" Is "doing good, good enough," or are we called to something more?

A SPECTRUM OF RESPONSES

Dietrich Bonhoeffer, in his 1928 lecture "Jesus Christ and the Essence of Christianity," gave a profound explanation of Christ's call to the lost. Christ demands an answer to one question: "Will you follow Me wholeheartedly or not all?" There is no room in the answer to mix our own causes with His.

Bonhoeffer went on to conclude that "Christianity preaches the unending worth of the apparently worthless and the unending worthlessness of what is apparently so valuable. The weak shall be made strong through God and the dying shall live."[5]

His comments reaffirmed that Christ and His relationship to us is all consuming and countercultural in its values and perspectives. When reading Bonhoeffer and those influenced by his writing, it is difficult to miss the point that Christ does not invite us to share our lives and agendas with Him, but rather to totally give our lives and agendas to Him.

Somewhat paradoxically, Bonhoeffer, who was resolutely focused on eternity and fundamentally committed to discipleship for the Christian, was executed in 1945 by the Nazis for his role in the revolutionary cause of overthrowing Hitler and the Nazi regime. In 1944, just prior to his execution and in preparation for a book, he observed that "the church is the church only when it exists for others. . . . To make a start, it could give away all its property for those in need."[6]

Bonhoeffer was doggedly committed to following Christ with an eternal perspective, but stood up for justice and the oppressed, making the investment that he believed was required of him—even to the point of death.

In his work *Ethics*, Bonhoeffer may have provided a solution to the dilemma he faced:

> The way of Jesus Christ, and thus the way of all Christian thought, is not the way from the world to God but from God to the world. This means that the essence of the gospel does not consist in solving worldly problems, and also that this cannot be the essential task of the church. However, it does not follow from this that the church would have no task at all in this regard. But we will not recognize its legitimate task unless we first find the correct starting point.[7]

Much like Bonhoeffer, Christians in the twenty-first century are confronted with the complexities of engaging the topic of social investment and the Christian life. On the one hand, we may be tempted to totally abandon social investment in furtherance of the message of salvation and resolutely focus on the pre-eminence of eternity, choosing to center on Christ's death and resurrection and the need for spiritual rebirth. On the other hand, we may be tempted to dilute, if not abandon, the gospel for the achievement of temporal social goods, choosing to focus on Christ's acts of love and call to care for the poor and needy.

Not many people would define themselves as being aligned with either extreme, but we are all somewhere on the spectrum between them. Some of us resist or diminish temporal engagement because we are focused on the call of Scripture to proclaim the gospel, and see this life as a mere momentary passing. Others resist the gospel and the scriptural implications of death, heaven, and hell, and focus instead on the good that can be done on earth by being living illustrations of God's great love.

The New Testament undeniably teaches that the concerns of a revisited social gospel—poverty, hunger, water, homelessness, medical epidemics, social justice, equality, and environmentalism—ought to be concerns of the redeemed. Social investment ought to be important to every follower of Christ because our love must emulate God's love and our lives must emulate Christ's life.

It is equally undeniable that the Scripture proclaims that Christ was and is principally concerned with eternity and the reconciliation of the lost. Fundamentally, Christ came to earth to seek and to save, not to heal and feed. Just as Christ came to provide the only means for spiritual reconciliation with the Father, He calls the redeemed to the specific task of continuing His ministry of reconciliation.

Jesus was a humanitarian, but of a unique kind. He healed to reveal true healing. He fed to reveal true food. He quenched thirst to reveal everlasting water. Christ's actions were temporal, but His intended impact was for His every word and deed to be eternally transforming.

Christ understood that His life and our lives are rooted in the freedom of spiritual eternity, not the slavery of physical time and circumstances. This is precisely why He was so focused on what was unseen, the things above. Either eternity hung in the balance of Christ's life, death, and resurrection, or it did not. Either eternity hangs in the balance for each of us, irrespective of the quality or durations of our lives, or it does not.

If it doesn't, then you should stop reading this book. But if it does, if our lives are merely a drop of water in the oceans of eternity, then perhaps we should ask ourselves in the realms of evangelism and social justice, "What on earth are we doing?"

Any religion which professes to be concerned about the souls of men and is not concerned about the social and economic conditions that scar the soul is a spiritually moribund religion only waiting for the day to be buried.

—MARTIN LUTHER KING JR.[1]

Chapter 2

SOCIALIZING
THE GOSPEL

Over the last ten to fifteen years, there have been few greater evangelists for the plight of the global poor and diseased than Bono. His rock-star celebrity and musical genius have perhaps only been paralleled by his commitment to resolve third world debt, global poverty, and the medical afflictions of Africa. He is unabashed in his discomfort with the lack of investment in these problems by the Christian church in general, and conservative evangelicals in particular.

Not a stranger to controversy, in his speech at the 2006 National Prayer Breakfast in Washington, D.C., Bono highlighted that as a self-proclaimed "believer" and student of Scripture, he made every effort to avoid religious people because of their indifference to the plight of humanity and use of God as a tool for self-indulgence, and to avoid religion because of its ability to "get in the way of God." Excerpted in part below, his speech made clear that Christ's religion lives in streets where the boots get "dirty":

Look, whatever thoughts you have about God, who He is or if He exists, most will agree that if there is a God, He has a special place for the poor. In fact, the poor are where God lives.

Check Judaism. Check Islam. Check pretty much anyone. I mean, God may well be with us in our mansions on the hill. I hope so. He may well be with us in all manner of controversial stuff. Maybe, maybe not. But the one thing we can all agree [on]—all faiths, all ideologies—is that God is with the vulnerable and poor.

God is in the slums, in the cardboard boxes where the poor play house. God is in the silence of a mother who has infected her child with a virus that will end both their lives. God is in the cries heard under the rubble of war. God is in the debris of wasted opportunity and lives, and God is with us if we are with them.[2]

While Bono was expressing his passion, he was also putting modern words to a long-standing idea that the call of Christianity is not just a call to evangelism but to social investment and reform.

Arriving at a full and historically accurate definition of the social gospel is beyond the scope of this book. However, before we can consider what we should think about the role of humanitarian investment in our lives, we should first understand what that terminology means and has meant.

LOOKING BACK

For the past 150 years or so, Christian scholars, pastors, authors, and laypeople have engaged and re-engaged the relationship between the biblical doctrines of gospel evangelism and social investment. The burning question is this: What are followers of Christ supposed to do in the realm of secular social issues such as poverty, hunger, homelessness, injustice, and oppression?

The basic issue is presented in the following hypothetical incident:

On an ordinary Sunday morning in a large church outside of Denver, a man stood up after the sermon was finished and interrupted the pastor. He was dirty and unkempt, obviously not well off. He started by saying, "I was just wondering, after your words today, pastor, what it really means to follow Jesus. You see, I came to this church last week for some food, but no one helped me. I stood on the corner by the light up the street before this service, and many of the people here drove past me on the way into the parking lot. Not one person stopped to offer anything; in fact, most of you looked the opposite way."

He went on to say, "I lost my job in a car factory nine months ago, my children have left me, and my wife died just last week. I don't blame you or God for any of this, but I get puzzled when I see so many Christians living in luxury and singing about following Jesus while so many suffer and die in this world. It's not just me; I read the papers about genocide and AIDS and the slums in our cities. There is suffering all over the world. I was just wondering, as I sat here in the back of this church, what it really means to follow Jesus. Pastor, you said that it was necessary to follow in Christ's steps, but what do Christians really mean by following the steps of Jesus? It seems to me that so many of the problems of this world could be solved if people like you actually got out of this church and tried to do something." The man finished and sat down.

This story highlights the basic problem of Christian indifference (at worst) or passivity (at best). Christianity and the life of Christ speak to ideals of love, suffering, compassion, and service; but at some level, churches and Christians have often been absent from the great social causes of mankind.

You might have recognized the above story. It could have happened in any number of churches across the world, but it is actually an adaptation of the beginning of Charles Sheldon's classic 1896 work *In His Steps,* in which he penned the famed question, "What would Jesus do?"[3]

Sheldon was one of the great fiction writers of the early social gospel period and accounts like this one captured the underlying ethos of the movement, highlighting the hypocritical gap between Christians' words and deeds.

At the most basic level, the social gospel asks Christians to be concerned and invested in the world around them. It asks Christians to have compassion for the hungry, concern for the sick, and empathy for the enslaved. The social gospel takes seriously the call of Scripture to care for widows and orphans, the destitute and the oppressed. It asks us to put our faith into action by taking seriously the needs of a broken, hurting world.

The German theologian Gerhard Uhlhorn in his 1881 text *Christian Charity in the Ancient Church* reasoned that the exercise of Christian charity flows out of our individual membership in, and the importance of, the kingdom of God on earth. Uhlhorn masterfully summarized the idea of expansive Christian charity and investment as follows:

> The Christian Church can never be conceived of as without charity: it was inherent in it from the very beginning. And it was so, not only because its Lord and Head taught love and commanded love, but because He Himself practiced it. He was not only a teacher of love, or a lawgiver of love, but His life was also the first example of a life of love. It was not the maxims which He uttered about it, nor the commandments which He gave, but the fact that in Him personally love was manifest, that moved by love He came to us, and lived upon earth a life which from its very first breath to its latest was spent in the service of love, and that He finally, through the greatness of His love, gave Himself for us to the death of the cross; that is the beginning and the never failing source of charity amid His followers. The beginning and the end of the history which we wish to narrate lies in these words of the Master: "The Son of man came not to be ministered unto, but to minister, and to give His life a ransom for many."[4]

Thus, for Uhlhorn, the social gospel or social Christianity is merely the expression of the Christian living as Christ did, lovingly invested in the world around Him.

At a more complex level the modern social gospel is a multifaceted theology expounded most notably by Walter Rauschenbusch, which gives central importance to the kingdom of God on earth and the Christian's role in bringing it to fruition. Stated differently, the social gospel is the application of Christ's teachings and the concept of salvation to all aspects of life—society, government, and individuals. It has taken the form of theology, policy, philosophy, and even political theory.[5]

Rauschenbusch, at the outset of his seminal 1907 work, *Christianity and the Social Crisis*, reflected that "social crisis is the overshadowing problem of our generation." His statement was as true for him in 1907 as it is for us today. He argued that Christianity's role was to transform society into the kingdom of God by bringing its institutions and communities into accordance with God's will. To him, this required repentance and confession of social sin by the individual and society, and faith in the possibility of a new social order.[6]

For some followers of the social gospel, men such as Josiah Strong, Charles Sheldon, Edward Beecher, and Washington Gladden, nothing less than the achievement of the full kingdom of God on earth was the target—"the kingdom of heaven brought down out of the skies to be realized progressively here and now."[7]

At watershed moments in American history (e.g., post–Civil War Reconstruction, the Industrial Revolution, the Great Depression, the Civil Rights movement, and perhaps in response to the Computer and Information Revolutions), Christians have attempted to respond to the circumstances and crises confronting humanity both regionally and globally. Whether or not these Christians upheld the full social gospel, their responses to suffering have typified the key concerns of leaders like Rauschenbusch and Gladden, namely, a deep desire to see our broken world made right.

CROSSING A GREAT DIVIDE

Nevertheless, for most of the social gospel's history, a great debate and resulting divide has raged within Christianity concerning the propriety of investing in a primarily social rather than spiritual gospel. Conservative evangelicals felt that it was a departure, a distraction of sorts, from the main work of proclaiming the gospel of salvation. Social gospellers maintained to varying degrees of extremity that the true call of Christ was to fulfill His kingdom goals and values on earth.

Expressing a conservative viewpoint in this debate, Liam Goligher, in his book *The Jesus Gospel*, explains that while Christ was kind to the weak and loving to the poor, the heart of the message of Scripture is that His death "changes the world for us." He writes,

> Confessing evangelicals are committed to acts of mercy, that is to social action and caring for people on a practical level, but church history shows how

easily the balance can swing away from gospel work to social work. Acts of mercy and charity are part and parcel of our general Christian responsibility to our neighbours and even our enemies. But the church on earth is "the pillar and buttress of truth" (1 Tim. 3:15) charged with defining, declaring and defending the gospel.[8]

Focusing on a more socially oriented gospel, on the other hand, Tony Campolo contends,

> I think that Christianity has two emphases. One is a social emphasis to impart the values of the kingdom of God in society—to relieve the sufferings of the poor, to stand up for the oppressed, to be a voice for those who have no voice. The other emphasis is to bring people into a personal, transforming relationship with Christ, where they feel the joy and the love of God in their lives.[9]

Goligher's and Campolo's thoughts well articulate the tension that has existed and continues to exist within the church regarding how we are to balance Christ's words and works. In the midst of this ongoing divide, two watershed moments of transition occurred between 1973 and 1975 that represented a reconciliation of sorts in the split between evangelism and social investment.

First, Ron Sider along with some fifty other evangelical leaders met in Chicago in 1973, formed the now-historic Evangelicals for Social Action group, and penned the Chicago Declaration, portions of which are set forth below:

> We acknowledge that God requires love. But we have not demonstrated the love of God to those suffering social abuses.

> We acknowledge that God requires justice. But we have not proclaimed or demonstrated his justice to an unjust American society. . . . We deplore the historic involvement of the church in America with racism and the conspicuous responsibility of the evangelical community for perpetuating the personal attitudes and institutional structures that have divided the body of

Christ along color lines. Further, we have failed to condemn the exploitation of racism at home and abroad by our economic system. . . .

We must attack the materialism of our culture and the maldistribution of the nation's wealth and services. We recognize that as a nation we play a crucial role in the imbalance and injustice of international trade and development. Before God and a billion hungry neighbors, we must rethink our values regarding our present standard of living and promote a more just acquisition and distribution of the world's resources. . . .

We proclaim no new gospel, but the Gospel of our Lord Jesus Christ who, through the power of the Holy Spirit, frees people from sin so that they might praise God through works of righteousness.

By this declaration, we endorse no political ideology or party, but call our nation's leaders and people to that righteousness which exalts a nation.

We make this declaration in the biblical hope that Christ is coming to consummate the Kingdom and we accept his claim on our total discipleship until he comes.[10]

This declaration and the growing perspective it recorded was followed in 1974 by the Lausanne Covenant. Over two thousand people from 150 nations representing all branches of the Christian church came together and adopted a document that included the idea that Christians needed to engage the issues of social justice and begin to reconcile the extreme positions that existed in the body. Section 5 of the Covenant, entitled "Christian Social Responsibility," declared the following (emphasis added):

We affirm that God is both the Creator and the Judge of all men. We therefore should share his concern for justice and reconciliation throughout human society and for the liberation of men and women from every kind of oppression. Because men and women are made in the image of God, every person, regardless of race, religion, colour, culture, class, sex or age, has an intrinsic dignity because of which he or she should be respected and served, not exploited. Here too we express penitence both for our neglect and for having sometimes regarded evangelism and social concern as mutually exclusive. *Although reconciliation with other people is not reconciliation with God, nor is social action evangelism, nor is political liberation salvation, nevertheless we affirm that evangelism and socio-political involvement are both part of our Christian duty. For both are necessary expressions of our doctrines of God and man, our love for our neighbour and our obedience to Jesus Christ.* The message of salvation implies also a message of judgment upon every form of alienation, oppression and discrimination, and we should not be afraid to denounce evil and injustice wherever they exist. When people receive Christ they are born again into his kingdom and must seek not only to exhibit but also to spread its righteousness in the midst of an unrighteous world. The salvation we claim should be transforming us in the totality of our personal and social responsibilities. Faith without works is dead.

Writing in 1975, John Stott, in his commentary to the section, noted that unlike the evangelical Christians of nineteenth-century Britain, evangelical Christians in the 1900s "tended to divorce evangelism from social concern" and concentrated "almost exclusively on the former." Stott cogently noted that "Christian duty arises from Christian doctrine. So this section is not content merely to assert that Christians have social responsibilities: it goes on to outline the four main doctrines out of which our Christian social duty springs, namely the doctrines of God, man, salvation and the kingdom."[11]

Both of these documents recognized that we are saved for eternity, but live in the momentary. We look forward to the completion of God's work of redemption, but live in a broken world that requires investment motivated by God's redemptive work in our lives.

Regardless of your precise understanding of this duality, both sides are at least in part biblical. Some of us feel more driven to emphasize one or the other, but we all must acknowledge that, biblically, they cannot be divorced.

LOOKING FORWARD

Today, a new form of "social gospel" appears to be emerging, perhaps straying from the fundamental biblical truths that undergirded the Chicago

Declaration and the Lausanne Covenant. This version of the social gospel can be understood to suggest that Christianity is almost exclusively encompassed by the concepts of "love" and "doing good." It accepts the second of the Great Commandments—love your neighbor as yourself—but makes little reference to the first—love your Lord God with all your heart, mind, and soul.

In the words of Rauschenbusch, it appears that "men are seizing on Jesus as the exponent of their own social convictions."[12] This emerging brand of Christianity stresses the need for global unity through love, justice, sacrifice, and kindness, but speaks less if at all of the ideas that divide—judgment, sin, heaven, hell, and the narrow road.

Princeton University secular ethicist Peter Singer in his 2009 book *The Life You Can Save* provides interesting insight into this emerging reality. "In the Christian tradition, helping the poor is a requirement for salvation." Singer also suggests that Christ in His teaching placed "far more emphasis on charity for the poor than on anything else" and traces this point from the early church to modern times, referencing the current work of Jim Wallis and Rick Warren in social causes.[13]

While theologically not true in the slightest regard—the Christian tradition has never taught that helping the poor is a requirement for salvation, but rather an evidence of it—Singer's reflections on what Christianity "is" may provide a view of what many think contemporary Christianity believes based on what publicly professing Christians are saying and doing.

If Singer's definition of Christianity is at all being accepted by mainstream thought or factions of Christian churches and charities, then it highlights the risk that we may be moving toward a merely social gospel, minus the biblical gospel.

On February 5, 2009, President Barack Obama gave an address at the National Prayer Breakfast. He shared that the roots of his personal faith came about in response to the call of God's "higher purpose" that he found in the work of social charity and concern carried out by the neighborhood churches of the south side of Chicago. Reflecting on the meaning of this purpose, President Obama stated,

No matter what we choose to believe, let us remember that there is no religion whose central tenet is hate. There is no God who condones taking the life of an innocent human being. This much we know.

We know too that whatever our differences, there is one law that binds all great religions together. Jesus told us to "love thy neighbor as thyself." The Torah commands, "That which is hateful to you, do not do to your fellow." In Islam, there is a hadith that reads, "None of you truly believes until he wishes for his brother what he wishes for himself." And the same is true for Buddhists and Hindus; for followers of Confucius and for humanists. It is, of course, the Golden Rule—the call to love one another; to understand one another; to treat with dignity and respect those with whom we share a brief moment on this Earth. . . .

Instead of driving us apart, our varied beliefs can bring us together to feed the hungry and comfort the afflicted; to make peace where there is strife and rebuild what has broken; to lift up those who have fallen on hard times. . . .

We come to break bread and give thanks and seek guidance, but also to rededicate ourselves to the mission of love and service that lies at the heart of all humanity.[14]

The remarks of President Obama are not unique because they invoke the role of Christianity and charity in American political life, but because they may be more generally reflective of the emergence of a new style of "American Christianity" focused solely on charity, unity, compassion, and social investment.

Two months after President Obama's remarks, Jon Meacham, editor of *Newsweek* magazine and an Episcopalian, in his April 13, 2009, cover story "The Decline and Fall of Christian America," sketched the contours of the religious landscape in which President Obama's remarks have found footing. Meacham, in reflecting on a post-Republican, post-Religious Right nation that is grappling with newly emerging definitions of Christianity and the role it can play in social and political life, noted the following:

Two thirds of the public (68 percent) now say religion is "losing influence" in American society, while just 19 percent say religion's influence is on the rise.

The proportion of Americans who think religion "can answer all or most of today's problems" is now at a historic low of 48 percent. During the Bush 43 and Clinton years, that figure never dropped below 58 percent.

Many conservative Christians believe they have lost the battles over issues such as abortion, school prayer and even same-sex marriage, and that the country has now entered a post-Christian phase.

If Meacham is correct and Obama's words are at all reflective of where "American Christianity" is heading in the next decade, it would represent a radical departure from the "American Christianity" of the Religious Right, which stressed morality and social conservatism, drawing sharp distinctions between "us" and "them." While such a shift might be refreshing and in many ways positive, it also presents a danger of overlooking those most basic truths of Christ's call that we must first die before we can live and that life eternal is far more significant than life here and now.

A BALANCED PERSPECTIVE

At its best, the social gospel asserts that the gospel, Jesus, and the kingdom of heaven on earth must influence our beliefs and actions in relation to our fellow humanity and creation. At its best, it represents a courageous cry for Christians to get out of their churches and into the streets, to invest in the here and now while we still can, and to be a visible expression of an invisible Savior.

It is unlikely that any reader has missed the growing number of opportunities to invest in Christian and secular humanitarian work around the globe. With the rise of ONE and other massive international awareness campaigns, we are inundated with information and opportunities. Numerous star athletes, celebrities, politicians, and companies have a cause and are able to mobilize millions of supporters.

In the Christian realm we can sponsor children, provide Bibles, fund clean water, support environmental causes, and invest ourselves in almost any form of charitable endeavour in the name of Christ. For many of us the question isn't *if* we should invest in social causes, but what causes to concentrate on. Missions funding is progressively being spread over a broader array of activities, ranging from pure evangelism to pure social relief.

On the whole, these are all positive developments. Christian investment in social justice causes should increase as we better understand the world around us. Peter Singer is right that we should act now to end the deplorable consequences of world poverty.[15]

But in tackling the global issues that face us today, we must wrestle with what good we should be doing and how we can be confident that our social investments will be commended by our Master with the words, "Well done, good and faithful servant."[16]

There are two ways to be fooled: One is to believe what isn't so; the other is to refuse to believe what is so.

—SØREN KIERKEGAARD

Chapter 3

THREE TRUTHS

Over the past one hundred years much has been written on the biblical foundation for making social investment in the world around us. Some of that writing was highlighted in the last chapter. In most cases, the questions for the individual boil down to arguments between the importance of sharing the gospel and investing in the lives of the lost. Is it better to give a tract or a sandwich to a hungry man? Which should be given to him first?

Over the course of my life I have volunteered in a few urban rescue missions. On one occasion, the mission required the homeless to attend a "church" service before being ushered into the dining hall. On a different occasion, the mission proclaimed that they were serving the homeless for Jesus, but His name never came up while I was there.

Is it right to share the gospel before giving someone a meal or a vaccine? Is it wrong to simply love an abused child in the name of God, but never explain what it really means that God loves her? Should we only support Christian humanitarian agencies, or is it okay to support mainstream humanitarian organizations doing the best work, regardless of their creed?

On a more personal level, is it wrong that I feel that God has empowered me to do more with my hands than with my words? What if God has called me to preach the gospel? Is one form of outreach more important than another?

These are the real questions we must struggle with and our answers depend on our understanding of what the Bible teaches is true about our condition, our actions, and our lives.

THREE IMPORTANT TRUTHS

While working on this book I had the chance to spend some time in Washington, D.C. While there I took a walk around the monuments on the Mall. I was struck by the formidable grandeur of our capital and the relative size I felt both in stature and in the span of American history. As part of my exploration I walked around the Washington Monument and, like a little boy, decided I needed to touch it.

I walked up to the monument, placed my hands flat against it, and looked up at the beautiful blue sky. As I pushed against the smooth stone I was filled with an awareness of my minuscule size and power relative to the monument. There I stood, pushing against the massive structure, in a strange way measuring myself against it. The Washington Monument was not going to fall or move because I pushed on it. In fact, aside from the sweat of my palms, it was totally unaffected.

I have repeated this little ritual all over the world and experienced the same sensation. When I push against something that is substantial, unwavering, and real, I am acutely aware of my own true size and substance, more so than when I simply exist in open space.

This to me is the essence of truth. Truth is what we push against, measure ourselves against, and hold on to, and in so doing, become acutely aware of who we really are, what we really think, and where our life is really going.

In 1828, Webster's Dictionary defined truth as "conformity to fact or reality; exact accordance with that which is, or has been, or shall be." Jesus defined truth in two words—"I am." Truth is the substance of God, that which originates from Him. It is the stuff of divinity. In our temporal existence filled with distortions and deception, truth is the fingerprint of our Creator left on the finish of His creation for us to discover.

Because our actions and beliefs can only be directed toward things that matter if we first come to terms with what those things are, the truth is vitally important. And so, when we come to issues as volatile and complex as humanitarian investment, the saving of lives and souls, we can debate and discuss all we want, but at the end of the day the only thing that really matters is the truth.

In relation to our discussion, three biblical truths seem vitally important to our decision making.

TRUTH 1: ETERNITY IS REAL

We are eternal beings, confined for a season to this physical reality, confronted with God's plan of redemption.

To begin, we need to realize that humans are eternal. Most world religions agree that there is some existence other than this physical existence in which we will continue. Assuming you don't believe that when you die the lights go out and nothing follows, you have some conception of what will happen after death.

Biblically, the story is quite clear. God knew you before the foundations of the earth were formed and He knit you together in your mother's womb. While she brought you into this world, He will take you out of it and you will continue to exist throughout eternity. Leaving aside the details, that eternal existence will take place either with or without the presence of God.

This may come as a surprise if you have always understood eternal life to mean that if you are saved by Christ you live forever with Him and if you are not, well, then your life just stops. This is not biblically accurate. Every human will live forever; the question is where and in what condition.[1]

Eternal life, then, is both a reality and a dilemma. The reality is that our physical life on this earth as we know it will last for a season. That season is undefined in length and experience, but we can be certain that we will physically live for only a season. And then we will die. This is the reality.

The dilemma is that our eternity is controlled by the decisions we make now. In God's plan we are given a choice to be with Him or to be without

Him. To live eternally in His presence or eternally separated from Him. But the offer expires when life expires.

For those who are reconciled to Christ, life on this earth will be the furthest we will ever be from Him. For those who are not, it is the closest. C. S. Lewis put it this way:

> But what you ask of earth? Earth, I think, will not be found by anyone to be in the end a very distinct place. I think earth, if chosen instead of Heaven, will turn out to have been, all along, only a region in Hell: and earth, if put second to Heaven, to have been from the beginning a part of Heaven itself.[2]

The reality of this life is that it is only a small part of reality. Each of us is working on a time clock that has no restart button. And so, it should come as no surprise that our eternal condition is a primary concern of Scripture.

In John chapter 6, after Christ fed the five thousand and walked on water, He decided to thin the crowd that was following Him by making His priority clear: It was eternal life that interested Him. "You have to eat my flesh to stop hungering; you have to feed on me if you want eternal life" (see John 6:53–54). The crowd wasn't interested in this idea. They weren't looking for eternal life, they were looking for temporal satisfaction of need. But Christ was interested in spiritual life because that is what His Father sent Him to bring forth (John 10:10).

Jesus continued the theme as he moved closer to the cross. "I am the light of the world, the living water, the One who can set you free in truth, the Good Shepherd that will lay down his life for you so that you can enter the door when I call."[3]

In case we missed it before, Christ made it clear that He exclusively was and remains the way, truth, and life; the one and only way to the Father; the resurrection and the life so that whoever believes in Him—though he dies—shall live.[4]

The point was not lost on the writers of the New Testament. Peter preached it at Pentecost, and after, Paul preached it everywhere, and John was captivated by it. The apostles and followers of Christ fervently proclaimed to all who would listen that today is the day of salvation, the world and its cares are passing away, and eternity demands a response to Christ's death, resurrection, presence, and purpose.[5]

Somewhat paradoxically, for all of the social investment made by Christ during His public ministry, the pages of the New Testament verify that the early church leaders spent the majority of their time preaching and teaching about Christ crucified and resurrected, and the eternal consequences of the decision to follow Him. In fact, relatively few instances of miraculous meetings of need or other general non-church mass humanitarian efforts can be found outside of what occurred at the outset of the church in Jerusalem and to substantiate the legitimacy of the apostles' message.[6]

There is no escaping this simple reality taught by Christ and emphasized by the apostles—you and I, and every other human on this earth will spend eternity in heaven with Christ or in hell without Him. This life has only two exits, and the one each of us chooses is of the greatest eternal importance.

TRUTH 2: TEMPORAL INVESTMENT IS IMPORTANT
Christ's life and teachings compel us to invest in the temporal problems of His creation.

The topic of this book would be easily covered, almost dismissed, if not for this truth. We could simply acknowledge the ministry of the message of salvation and seek to share that message. But this truth precludes such simplicity. There is such irresistible evidence of Christ's choice to solve temporal issues like sickness, hunger, oppression, and disease that we cannot set it aside as if it were a divine afterthought.

When Christ entered His creation, He knew that the world around Him didn't work the way He had designed it. He had not created human beings to suffer or His creation to waste away. He had not created disease and drought, hate and violence. He created us to be in communion with Him and with His creation. He created us with something totally different in mind. Christ knew that the world around Him bore little resemblance to what His Father intended. And as a result, God incarnate healed, fed, and spoke unlike any other human in history.

There can be no escaping the truth that Christ walked the earth healing, feeding, touching, loving, and restoring a glimpse of what He had intended. The Gospels record well over thirty instances where Christ healed or fed a single individual, multiple people, or the masses.

Even a cursory reading of the Gospels reveals the immense investment Christ made in His creation while He walked the earth. Setting aside the miracles He performed to reveal His divinity or fulfill specific prophecy, there remains an abundance of examples of social investment by our Master.[7]

At the outset, after spending some time in the wilderness, Jesus calls Simon Peter and Andrew to follow Him, and then goes throughout all of Galilee "healing every disease and every affliction among the people." He performed such great acts of miraculous mercy that large crowds came to Him from an expansive area.[8]

When He finished preaching the Sermon on the Mount, He continued healing the paralyzed, sick, diseased, and oppressed.

Even on His way to Jerusalem to die for the sins of mankind, He stopped to heal the blind man, as we discussed in chapter 1.[9]

But Christ didn't just live the example of humanitarian investment and compassion, He taught it. He gave us the second Great Commandment, Love your neighbor as yourself, and then He gave us the parable of the good Samaritan to define who our neighbors are and how we should love them. He also taught us to love our enemies, to share ourselves with those we don't know, to lay up our treasures in heaven rather than on earth, and to give our riches to the poor.[10]

Despite the fact that Christ didn't feed, heal, or touch everyone—and in fact frequently left crowds, turned away seekers, and left sick, broken people in their sickness—He clearly taught us to invest in our fellow humans, to love them as we love ourselves, and to give ourselves away, and He lived out an example for us to follow.[11]

We could move on to examine other teachings of the Old and New Testaments that also support this truth, but if you don't accept what Christ did and said, then you won't be swayed by those teachings either.

In short, if you don't believe Christ is calling you to love, serve, and invest in the world around you and those suffering under sickness, poverty, disease, and injustice—you are just dead wrong.

TRUTH 3: EVERY SERVANT HAS A MASTER
Every Christian is called to serve Christ in His continuing work of reconciling the lost to Himself.

Every Christian is a servant. That is part of the deal. We don't add Christ to our lives; we give Him our lives as servants, and He becomes our Master. This necessarily creates within each of us an enduring question: "What is my Master's will for my life?"

In a bigger sense, every Christian is faced with two questions. "Why am I here?" and "Why am I *still* here?" We say to ourselves, "I get it. God saved me. I am a new creation. I have new meaning and cause. But why am I still here? Is this life just about 'being a Christian'? Is it just about waiting around for the end, trying to rack up good works?"

In one sense we could answer these questions by tracing the answers given in Scripture. This would result in us learning that as servants we are to be thankful, to persevere in suffering and tribulation, to walk worthy of our calling, to love each other, and so on. These are all very true, but they are all streams that flow from one great river: we are here to serve Christ in His continuing appeal to the lost for reconciliation.

Christ in His very existence was a divine appeal. He drew people to Himself. He told them that He was the way, the truth, and the life. He offered them salvation and in exchange asked them to count the cost. He fed some, healed some, and raised some from the dead, and as He did that, He told them about living water, living food, and life eternal.

But Christ has departed the earth. He is at the right hand of the Father. He is no longer making a physical appeal on this earth to the lost, but His servants should be. We should be making that appeal because that is the way God designed it.

Charles Spurgeon said it this way (emphasis mine):

If God had willed it, each of us might have entered heaven at the moment of conversion. It was not absolutely necessary for our preparation for immortality that we should tarry here. . . . Had the Lord so willed it, He might have changed us from imperfection to perfection, and have taken us to heaven at once. Why then are we here? . . . The answer is—*[We] are here [to] "live unto the Lord," and . . . bring others to know His love. We remain on earth as sowers to scatter good seed; as ploughmen to break up the fallow ground; as heralds publishing salvation. We are here as the "salt of the earth," to be a blessing to the world. We are here to glorify Christ in our daily life. We are here as workers for Him, and as "workers together with Him."* Let us see that our life answereth its end. Let us live earnest, useful, holy lives, to "the praise of the glory of His grace."[12]

Paul makes our calling abundantly clear when he states the following in 2 Corinthians 5:14–21 (emphasis mine):

> For the love of Christ controls us, because we have concluded this: that one has died for all, therefore all have died; and he died for all, that those who live might no longer live for themselves but for him who for their sake died and was raised.
>
> From now on, therefore, we regard no one according to the flesh. Even though we once regarded Christ according to the flesh, we regard him thus no longer. Therefore, if anyone is in Christ, he is a new creation. The old has passed away; behold, the new has come. All this is from God, who through Christ reconciled us to himself and gave us the ministry of reconciliation; that is, in Christ God was reconciling the world to himself, not counting their trespasses against them, and entrusting to us the message of reconciliation. Therefore, we are ambassadors for Christ, *God making his appeal through us.* We implore you on behalf of Christ, be reconciled to God. For our sake he made him to be sin who knew no sin, so that in him we might become the righteousness of God.

Christ came into the world. He died, He rose, He ascended, and now He is making an appeal to the lost through those He has redeemed.

Even before Paul laid out the reality of our calling, he focused his readers on the importance of an eternal perspective by explaining that this life is a tent, an earthly home, and that the things that are seen are transient, but the things that are not seen are eternal. While we are wasting away like clay pots and the earth is wasting with us, both we and the creation are groaning for eternity.[13]

And so Paul makes his focus obvious—the appeal. Not just the appeal he was personally making, but the appeal God is making through the redeemed. The word in the original is *parakaleo*, which actually means "to call to one's side; to call for; to summon." The word being used applies to every type of a call to a person designed to produce a result.[14]

Christ's appeal is not a halfhearted request. It is not a polite invitation given without a purpose—a "Hey, call me," or "We should get coffee." It is a summons, a passionate, striving call. It literally means to beg.

When Christ walked the earth, He experienced this kind of appeal firsthand. He experienced passionate, emotional, heart-wrenching calls. These were precisely the appeals—*parakaleo*—that were made over and over again when He was approached for a miracle by his hurting, broken, and suffering creation.[15] As Christ walked the earth, people implored Him for the chance to touch the fringe of His garment, they pleaded with Him to heal their servants, they begged Him to be healed from leprosy, and they earnestly called Him to heal their children.

And while they appealed for His healing touch, He in turn appealed to them to be reconciled. And He still does. God, our creator, is in fact pleading for His creation to come to Him. That is why, in the final analysis, God is not asking us to fix His creation. He is not asking us to just help His creation. He is not asking us to simply emulate His actions. He is calling people to Himself through us.

TRUE EVANGELISM

Question: Of the three truths discussed above, how many deal with evangelism?

The answer of course depends on what you believe the term *evangelism* means. When we picture an evangelist we often think of John the Baptist, Billy Graham, or a man standing on a corner calling out to the passersby to repent and believe.

Is evangelism sharing the gospel with someone? Is it sharing a tract or the four spiritual laws of salvation? Is the point of evangelism to have someone pray a prayer, walk down an aisle, or raise a hand?

Perhaps the most frequent and serious critique of social Christianity or the social gospel is that it ignores the call to evangelism. A staunch opponent to Christian social investment might argue that despite Christ's clear words and deeds, feeding a man's body without sharing the gospel of salvation is a departure from God's call for the church and His followers. The argument might continue that social causes are distractions from this pure work of evangelism and that we should be wary of such distractions.

This critique, while reasonable, presupposes a specific idea of what we mean when we say *evangelism*.

Is it possible to understand evangelism in such a way that it envelops both the physical and the spiritual? Did Christ provide us an example of what He believed evangelism should look like?

A traditional definition of evangelism would be the sharing of the gospel. To evangelize is to preach the gospel in an effort to convert hearers to believe.[16]

So is Billy Graham an evangelist? Yes. Is it evangelism when we share the truth of salvation with someone? Yes. But is it also evangelism when we care for the sufferings of a person on behalf of Christ? Yes.

Christ was an evangelist. His every effort was to draw people to Himself and to life only He could provide. This didn't stop when He fed or healed. He didn't believe these acts were departures from His evangelism, but part of it.

If we follow Christ's example, evangelism is not just sharing the gospel of salvation, and it is not just meeting needs. In fact, it is neither of those things. Evangelism is allowing Christ to so live in and through us that who we are, what we do, and what we say become the very expression of who He is, what He did, and what He said.

Evangelism includes the sharing of the gospel and the meeting of needs. It includes the challenging of injustice and the championing of the oppressed. The truth of evangelism is that each of our everlasting destinies is of such absolute importance that we should stop at nothing to ensure that everyone we meet, meets Christ.

Christ's evangelism was an appeal to the lost and broken. He drew them to Himself. And this hasn't changed. He hasn't stopped caring about the needs of the world that surrounded Him when He walked this earth, so neither can we. Christ didn't meet needs and live amongst the people just so He could have the chance to evangelize. He met needs and lived amongst the dying because that was itself part of the truth of evangelism. He called the weary and weak to come to Him. He offered Himself to them.

Likewise, we don't meet needs because it gives us the chance to share Christ, but because it is part of who Christ is, and if He is in us, it is part of who we are. We are not just sharing a message but reflecting the One who sends it. Christ reflected His Father in who He was, what He said, and what He did.[17] In the same way, we should reflect Christ in all that we are, say, and do.

When we define evangelism as just what we say, as a verbal call that requires a response, we improperly segregate it from who we are and what we do. But if we define it just as what we do and segregate it from who Christ is and what He said, then we forget that while Christ existed with people and met their needs, He called for a response. He called people to follow Him. To take up their cross and leave behind their lives.[18]

We have a Master and He is calling us to live in such a way that the world is evangelized—so that every human is confronted with Christ and offered the chance to accept His sacrifice and surrender to His Lordship.

The three truths of this chapter are all part of Christ's evangelism. We can't accept one and reject another. We can't choose to live one and not the others. If we believe these three truths then we must be committed to Christ's call in our lives to true ambassadorship that takes seriously the physical and spiritual realities of everyone we meet.

Everybody won't be treated all the same . . .

When the man comes around.

—JOHNNY CASH

"The Man Comes Around"

Chapter 4

LAST-BREATH
EQUALITY

One of the great complexities of life and our understanding of faith is that we can't consider issues or choices in isolation because very few things are absolute. When two ideas are important and we are asked to choose between them, we frequently face a dilemma.

From an ethical perspective we consider this concept in the game of "Lifeboat." Who is more important, the brain surgeon, the teacher, or the criminal? Loser gets tossed overboard. In mathematics, we talk about greater than, less than, or equal to. In everyday life, examples abound—my left and right eyes have equal importance, but my right hand is more important than my left. My wife is more important to me in every respect than my dog is. If pressed, I would tell you that I like Italian food more than Mexican food. My right to vote is important to me, but not as important as my right to be free from cruel and unusual punishment or unjust imprisonment. The ideas of justice and grace are both important to me, but I would rather have grace than receive justice.

Obeying the speed limit is right. Most of us don't do it for various reasons, but we all know it is right. However, when my son was seriously sick in the middle of the night and I needed to get to the emergency room as fast as possible, his health was more important than the speed limit.

I hate single-serving plastic bottles because we use billions of them a year, we recycle only two out of ten of them, and the rest end up in the ocean or a landfill. I don't think they should be used, but if I was pressed to send clean water to a village in Africa either in small plastic bottles or not at all, I would say, "Bring on the bottles."

If you play this game for even a few minutes, you will quickly find that very few things in your life, people you know, or ideas that you believe in, are equal. In most cases, if you were really pressed, you would say that one thing, passion, idea, pursuit, or person is more important than another.

THE DILEMMA OF THEN AND NOW

At the root of our discussion we find eternity and the relationship between the now and the tomorrow for each of us. We live in the temporal but our choices frequently impact the eternal. There is a simple fact that brings this into focus—we are all dying, one breath at a time. We want to believe that we will live on through the years, but when faced with the truth, we know there is no guarantee that we will make it through another minute.

Our lives are filled with twenty-four hours of near misses each day, often marked by what could have happened but didn't. Whether it is the freak occurrence of a plane crash or the more frequent traffic accident, we live with the knowledge that this day could be our last.

For those who live on the edge of oblivion, in famine-starved lands or war-torn cities, the reality of death is far more present. For most of us in developed nations, we can avoid it. We can quickly put out of mind that another's cancer could have been ours or that the near-fatal accident of a relative could have been deadly. We do everything we can to avoid the topic of death, even in the presence of the dead. We live with the knowledge of mortality, but behave as if it has no application to us. We are not wired to serve two masters, so we choose to serve the now and leave tomorrow to the Lord.

But Christ's call will not allow such service. We are called to be eternally focused on the preeminence of Christ's work of redemption, recognizing that we are citizens of His kingdom, while at the same time fully invested in the temporal conditions of this world.

R. C. Sproul put it this way:

One thing that indisputably has been lost from our culture is the idea that human beings are privately, personally, inexorably accountable to God for their lives. Imagine what would happen if suddenly the lights came on and everyone in the world said, "Hey, someday I will stand before my Maker, and I will have to give an account for every word that I have spoken, every deed that I have done, every thought that I have thought, and every task that I have failed to do. I am accountable."[1]

In the face of such accountability, how can we focus, as Johnny Cash so aptly put it, on the fact that the "Man" is "going to come around," while at the same time expending our energies and resources on temporal matters that might not matter on that day? Are Christian humanitarian investment and the work of orally sharing the gospel equal? Is it simply a matter of switching between them in some cosmic game of eeny-meeny-miny-moe?

Christ gave us a glimpse of how He dealt with these issues. When Peter challenged Him to avoid the cross, He called him Satan and told him to get behind Him. Why? Because unlike Christ, who was focused on the things of eternity, Peter was focused on the issues and conditions that faced him and his people on this earth.[2]

When Christ was tempted in the desert, He wasn't distracted by the things that mattered on this earth; He was focused on the things that mattered in heaven and His Father's will. When he met the woman at the well, it was living water that He was offering, not the kind we can get out of the ground. When He hung on the cross, He responded to the eternal need of the thief, not his physical need. And when He was lost by His parents and found in the temple, it was His Father's will He was about, not the agenda of His parents on earth.[3]

Christ made clear in His teachings that the inside is more important than the outside. God sees our hearts, and the work of the Lord *in* our lives is more important than the works *of* our lives, and the things that will last for eternity are more important than things that won't.[4]

This doesn't mean that how we live and what we choose to do or not to do, doesn't matter—that would be a cop-out—but it does mean that we must always view our temporal endeavors in light of the reality of eternity and the fact that we will all stand before the Savior at the moment of our last breath.

LAST-BREATH EQUALITY

Our world is largely marked by inequality. Jean-Jacques Rousseau, before penning some of the works that influenced the formation of American political thought, wrote his discourse on the inequality of man in the 1750s and ruminated that inequality ". . . derives its force and its growth from the development of our faculties and the progress of the human mind, and finally becomes fixed and legitimate through the institution of property and laws."[5] Rousseau was correct at least in this: as mankind has progressed, inequality has become largely inescapable.

Walter Rauschenbusch found the roots of the social crises of his time in this fact as well. He observed that humankind had always suffered under the dangers of nature and other people, and concluded that "social misery" had always existed because "the really grinding and destructive enemy of man is man."[6]

As much as we strive for equality, it does not exist. In the simplest terms, you and I have never been equal. We were not equal at our births and will not be equal in our lives. We can measure our inequality in health, talent, IQ, opportunity, compassion, skill, wealth, years, rights, blessings, or afflictions. No matter the measure, true equality can never be achieved in life. But it is always achieved at death.

There is absolute equality in our last breath because we all will be in the exact same situation. Our lungs will take in a last measure of air, our cells will receive their last oxygen, our heart will beat one last time, and our brains will shut off. The cause of our last breaths will be different, but the moment and all that it represents will occur just the same for you as for me.

Whether we talk about clinical death as the cessation of blood circulation and breathing or brain death as the irreversible end of all brain activity, we will all experience the exact same biological final moment, and in our last breath, for a moment in time, we will be equal.

Depending on who you ask, about 1.8 people die every second in the world, so chances are, when I die, someone, somewhere, will die at the exact same time. It will not matter whether that person and I die of AIDS, heart attack, starvation, or malaria. It will not matter whether we lived in plenty or want. It will not matter whether we suffered injustice or inflicted injustice upon others. In that moment, regardless of every single point of difference in our lives, we will be in exactly the same position.

A popular bumper sticker used to say, "The man who dies with the most toys still dies." This is absolutely true. Solomon, the richest, wisest, most cosmopolitan man in history declared that wealth was all vanity. Presumably he realized that he could not take it with him beyond the grave.[7] We can spend our lives amassing wealth and power, but those things will not follow us into eternity.

The man who dies with the most toys still dies . . . but, of course, the man who dies with no toys at all dies too.

The concept of death as the great leveler has often been used to argue against materialism, but it is equally true in cases of want and deprivation. If it doesn't matter how healthy or fit you are at death, it also doesn't matter how sick you are. If your wealth doesn't get buried with you, neither does your poverty. Solomon said that it was all vanity, all vanity—which excludes nothing and includes everything. It wasn't just the excess that was vanity; it was the good and the bad, the high and the low, the plenty and paucity. Solomon realized that death is the great leveler of all that can be done "under the sun" and when we reach that end, we will each face God and be held accountable.[8]

The inescapable reality for those who believe in final physical death and eternal existence as described in the Bible, is that it makes no difference what your physical, temporal circumstances are when you reach your last breath—they won't survive that moment.

No matter what we do in this life to improve our condition or the condition of mankind in general, it will all be rendered meaningless at the last breath of equality, unless what we did reaches into eternity.

This idea is simple to grasp, but hard to integrate into our lives. C. S. Lewis masterfully described the problem in the voice of Screwtape, the senior devil, detailing the hope of Satan for every believer:

> Prosperity knits a man to the World. He feels that he is "finding his place in it," while really it is finding its place in him. His increasing reputation, his widening circle of acquaintances, his sense of importance, the growing pressure of absorbing and agreeable work, build up in him a sense of being really at home in earth, which is just what we want.[9]

How at home on this earth are you? Have you found your place here? Are you primarily trying to help others find their place here or increase their prosperity? The more we focus on this life, the more it finds its place in us. We begin to look at things in isolation. We forget that we are all dying one breath at a time.

When we reach our last breath of equality, it will last one solitary moment in the span of eternity. Whatever happened before that in our human condition, in our circumstances and trials, will be done. The chapters of our physical lives will be closed and the chapters of eternity will come into focus.

Perhaps this seems obvious to you. Perhaps you are thinking, "Of course I can't do anything to help a poor or sick person after he is dead." "Of course the amount of money I have when I die won't matter to me." "Of course my temporal concerns won't follow me into eternity."

But ask yourself this question: If you can do nothing to help someone after their last breath of equality, what importance can there be for investments and efforts made on their behalf that don't reach into eternity?

If your efforts help a person out of poverty and sickness, out of affliction or abuse, out of hunger or homelessness, but don't attempt to reconcile them to God, then have you done anything of eternal value for them?

In one phase of my legal career I represented a man on death row in California in an effort to get him a new trial. I spent three years investigating and researching his life, the crimes he allegedly committed, and the legal issues involved. At the end of that time I filed over one thousand pages of documents in the California Supreme Court, arguing that he deserved a new series of trials. In a very real sense, I was standing between him and his last breath. The point of that work was very clear—to save him from execution, not to improve his life while on the way there.

Before I was a lawyer I was a state beach lifeguard. I rescued people every day who were drowning. I swam out, grabbed hold of them, and swam them to shore. That was my job. But what if I swam out and offered them a brief rest, remarking that they seemed tired from the struggle, and then left them to continue their struggle while I returned to shore? Surely, I would have been justifiably fired.

The point is this. Christ's work of physical redemption—His sacrificial love shown during His life by meeting physical needs—was important, but it was important because it was tied to His work on the cross. Christ did a lot of "good" things, He said a lot of "good" things, but none of His deeds in life would have made any eternal difference to humanity had they not been tied to eternity through His work of redemption on the cross and beyond the grave. Christ's temporal existence pointed people to His eternal reality.

We either believe in eternity or we don't. We either believe that heaven and hell are the two inescapable alternatives after life or we don't. If we do, then we must invest in things that are going to make an eternal difference.

Feeding a person's stomach is good, but connecting that work in evangelism that includes impacting his life such that Christ can feed his soul is better. Preventing the causes of physical death is good, but passionately investing in a life to prevent spiritual death at the same time is better.

We get it wrong if we say that doing "good" is "not good." We get it wrong if we say that serving mankind and creation isn't a worthwhile part of our evangelism, but rather somehow a departure from spirituality. It is good. But we also get it wrong if we don't realize that "doing good isn't good enough" unless it is tied to eternity.

Consider one last example. Picture yourself walking down a long hallway on the twentieth floor of a luxury hotel. You reach the elevator and wait for it to open. It arrives, you start to step in, but then notice that the doors are open and there is no elevator car—just an open shaft dropping twenty floors. You gasp and step back, noticing a sign adjacent to the door, warning that the elevator is broken. The doors close and you turn around and head toward the elevator at the other end of the four-hundred-yard-long hall, thinking about the near-miss of your life.

About halfway down the hall, a blind man in a business suit quickly walks toward you with a white cane, muttering about being late for a meeting. You notice that the man's dress shoes are untied, so you stop and say, "Sir, your shoes are untied; I don't want you to trip as you hurry to your meeting." Because he is blind and his hands are full, you stoop to tie his shoes. The businessman is shocked at the kindness and thanks you for both the warning and your generous actions. "I am in such a hurry—big meeting today with the bankers, thanks so much for the help."

You shake hands and go your separate ways. When you reach the lobby several minutes later, you notice a commotion near the other elevator and overhear that a blind businessman just fell to his death in an open elevator shaft. Upon hearing this, you think to yourself, "Wasn't it a good thing that his shoes were tied tight? At least he didn't trip."

On one level this story is unbelievably absurd. On another, it is exactly what we do when we tend to a person's temporal suffering and ignore their eternal, spiritual danger. The blind man was failed and deceived in what he believed was kindness. You, despite your beautiful act of service, actually withheld the vital warning that could have radically changed the businessman's destiny.

Here is the reality of Scripture. Heaven and hell hang in the balance of our relationship with Christ. Our evangelism, therefore, must express every aspect of Christ's character and concerns, both temporal and eternal.

We can hurt for the dying, minister to the starving, battle for the afflicted, and strive for the forgotten just as Christ did. But we can do nothing for them after their last breath of equality. It is appointed once for a man to die and then to face his Creator (Hebrews 9:27).

There are people in the world who are wasting away under the ravages of sin and oppression. They need people to invest in them—physically, emotionally, and spiritually. But that investment ought to reap its full reward on the other side of last-breath equality.

Just as the rich man in Jesus' parable could do nothing for his brothers after reaching eternity, we can do nothing of eternal value for the lost unless we seek that they be found in this life.[10]

The powerful play goes on and you may contribute a verse.

What will your verse be?

—WALT WHITMAN AND MR. KEATING, *DEAD POETS SOCIETY*

Chapter 5

GOSPEL-ROOTED
HUMANITARIANISM

As Christians, we must make humanitarian investment because God cares about human suffering. He so loved the world that He gave His Son to be the Savior of His created humanity. He cares that His perfect creation, the first revelation of His character, has been corrupted under the weight of sin. He cares. But He cares in the context of His absolute plan of redemption.

If I save a species of fish because a population depends on it, I have loved them. If I clean the ocean so that the unsaved can observe the presence of God revealed in nature, I have preserved a source of divine revelation. If I donate to AIDS relief, I show compassion rather than hate to communities that have been disenfranchised. If I try to eradicate poverty, I make investment in the world that can be correlated to God's investment in me and all mankind.

Christians must invest, but social investment, in whatever form that takes, can never be the single or primary focus of our lives. It must be rooted in our understanding of the gospel of salvation, the good news that this life is not all that exists, that the God who created us sent His Son to die for us so that we might be reconciled eternally with Him. Our work must always be rooted in the understanding that all of mankind is suffering under both the physical and spiritual consequences of brokenness.

When we are rooted in this knowledge, we can step outside of traditional walls and engage our culture and the world as Christ leads. The results of this kind of humanitarianism, Christ's humanitarianism, are transformative. Here are a few.

WE FOCUS ON PEOPLE, NOT PROBLEMS

Christ was right when He said the poor will always be with us, because poverty is a symptom of a fallen world. Poverty is a social problem, but a poor person is not. In the same way, the problems of sickness, hunger, and racism will always be with us—but a poor, hungry, racially disenfranchised person will not. She has a limited number of days on this earth during which we can help her, and then she will face eternity.[1]

One of the great risks of humanitarianism apart from the gospel is that it can focus on issues rather than people. People are eternal, issues are not. While Christ occasionally spoke about social issues, He most frequently dealt with individual people.

The problems of this world need solutions, but the people of this world need salvation. When we focus on people rather than problems, we focus on where Christ spent His life.

WE REMAIN ETERNALLY MINDED

One of the risks of an eternal mind-set is that we check out on this life. As Christians we can be guilty of adopting an "us-versus-them" mentality, reminding ourselves that this world is not ours and that we are citizens of another land.

These ideas are true. But the point is not that our circumstances are irrelevant. The point isn't that we can simply tell people that "God has a wonderful plan for their lives" so they shouldn't worry about how rotten their circumstances are. That is not biblical, eternal thinking.

Eternal thinking is realizing that our circumstances matter to God, but they matter in the context of eternity. It is realizing that this life and how we physically and emotionally experience it is not all there is. When we invest ourselves in the world, we should always remember that our investment must have an opportunity for eternal consequence in addition to its worthwhile temporal impact.

When we think with an eternal mind, we can evaluate "importance" by a different standard. During law school my wife and I moved to Ireland for a summer of study. We rented a house in Dublin and set up a life. But the life we set up was temporary. We knew we would be leaving that life in a couple of months, so we focused on different things. We didn't make improvements to our house. We didn't buy furniture or worry about the comfort of our beds. We didn't worry about the economy of Ireland or its politics. We didn't put things off or wait to do things until the weekend.

We lived deeply and totally immersed ourselves in the culture, people, and places. We met new friends and built relationships with an incredible intensity. We travelled every weekend, stayed out late every night, and got up early every morning. Our goal was to squeeze every ounce of experience and impact out of our time that we could.

The knowledge that we were sojourners living in a foreign land for a short period and that our citizenship was of a different country didn't make us less invested, it made us more invested, but with a different perspective and set of values.

In the same way, when we have an eternal perspective on this life, we invest differently than when we begin to live like and think that this is our home. Because we are called to have an eternal perspective, we should never focus primarily on that which is not eternal. Because our citizenship is not here, we must be careful to guard against building a home where we should only erect a tent.

Does this mean we should do nothing that helps people merely in the here and now, that everything we think, do, and say must be tied explicitly to eternity? No. But it does create a focus that allows our decision-making process to be based on biblical principles. Every once in a while it is important to stop and ask, "Is what I am doing today going to last into eternity?"

WE REMEMBER THAT GOD IS GOD AND WE ARE NOT

The gospel of salvation compels us to say, I am not, I cannot, I need everything. It requires us to realize our ultimate need for Christ and our inability outside of Him to please God.

The social gospel has the potential to say, I am important, I can make a difference, we can fulfill our neighbors' needs. Out of focus, the social gospel can place too much importance on man's abilities and efforts, thereby reducing God to a cosmic onlooker, hopeful that we can cure the consequences of sin.

In this light, saving a specific fish, finding a cure for AIDS, or ending global poverty, is not, in the biblical sense, of absolute and independent importance for the Christian.

God could intervene in His creation anytime, and, for example, save that species of fish if He so chose. After all, He created the fish, sustains the fish (as He sustains our lives), and could presumably, being the all-powerful Creator, supernaturally intervene and preserve the species. This same simple fact holds true for every other social issue, injustice, and torment. God could, if He chose to, fix what is broken on this earth. The fact that He probably won't do so during our lives does not negate the possibility or the importance of remembering that He could, and that there is a difference between creation and the Creator.

The biblical paradigm for fixing the brokenness of this earth is not by human endeavor through progressive restoration or renovation, but rather by divine re-creation.[2] When we lose sight of God's power and fixate on our power, we inevitably elevate ourselves beyond what is justifiable. This does not mean that we can't do great things through God's power, but it does mean that we must remember whose power it is.

On a related note, when we remember that God is God and we are not, we can better communicate God's love and compassion for the world in a way that it is God who is seen rather than us.

Consider the reaction of the crowd to Christ's encounter with a paralytic described in Luke 5:18–26.

Some men were bringing on a bed a man who was paralyzed, and they were seeking to bring him in and lay him before Jesus. . . . And when he saw their faith, he said, "Man, your sins are forgiven you." And the scribes and the Pharisees began to question, saying, "Who is this who speaks blasphemies? Who can forgive sins but God alone?" When Jesus perceived their thoughts, he answered them, "Why do you question in your hearts? Which is easier, to say, 'Your sins are forgiven you,' or to say, 'Rise and walk'? But that you may know that the Son of Man has authority on earth to forgive sins"—he said to the man who was paralyzed—"I say to you, rise, pick up your bed and go home." And immediately he rose up before them and picked up what he had been lying on and went home, glorifying God. And amazement seized them all, and they glorified God and were filled with awe, saying, "We have seen extraordinary things today."

On the one hand the crowd's reaction was understandable awe and amazement, taking note of the extraordinary things they had seen in Christ's compassionate healing. On the other hand, the crowd missed the point. Christ didn't really want them to walk away talking about the extraordinary things they had seen but rather the extraordinary person they had met. He was challenging them to realize that His power to forgive sin and create eternal relationship was far more important than His power to heal. He wanted them to meet God, not just experience His power.

In the same way, we should never be satisfied if the people we serve walk away talking about our extraordinary actions or what amazing people we are. They should leave having been touched by an extraordinary God who has the power not just to minister to their needs, but to forgive their sins.

When we remember that God is God and we are not, we can direct the eyes of the people we serve to Him rather than to us. Gandhi famously said, "Be the change you want to see in the world," a great idea in general, but not quite right for the Christian. We will never be the change we want to see in the world; Christ was and is that change in and through us. There is a difference. You and I are not going to change the world no matter who we are; but we can serve Christ in His work of changing the world because of who He is.

WE SERVE OUR MASTER AS HE DESIRES

One of the troubling things about living as a Christian is that you don't get to be the master. You have to take orders, regardless of your opinion.

The Bible is pretty clear on this. We are bond servants, bought with a price, redeemed for God's pleasure to serve Him on this earth. As a true servant, we do the Master's bidding, not because it benefits us, but because it benefits Him. Christ modeled this when He made clear that He was on earth not to do His own will but the work His Father sent Him to do.[3]

Christianity isn't a multiple-choice question where more than one answer is correct. You can't have two masters and you can't divide your allegiance. God the Father doesn't negotiate. His Son was sacrificed to offer redemption to mankind, and He rightly deems that sacrifice sufficient to unilaterally set the terms by which we can accept His gift.[4]

There may be nothing more difficult for the Christian to comprehend than this fact. You might be doing great work for God, but if it is not the work He is calling you to perform, then you need to do something about it because you might be succeeding in the wrong things.

The reality of a "Christianity" that merely consists of doing human-directed and human-empowered good works, detached from the gospel of salvation, is that it is un-offensive to the world and to ourselves. There are few people anywhere who would have taken issue with Mother Teresa for her work with the poor or a Christian investing in the needy. We could spend an entire life serving people and never once risk offending anyone.

But if we open our mouths and share the biblical gospel of salvation, then we risk offense, humiliation, and scorn. We risk being called unloving, narrow-minded, and intolerant. We risk being persecuted rather than praised.

We would rather do anything for Christ than open our mouths and share the good news of salvation. But that is not good enough, nor will it be an acceptable answer to Christ when we reach our last breath of equality.

Christ opened His mouth and the apostles did the same. The consequences for almost all of them were severe, but if you asked any of them, they would confirm it was worth it. Our evangelism must include what we do and who we are, but it must also include words.

WE LIVE WHERE WE BELONG

Awash in blood, sweat, and tears is the purest place the gospel can be found. The good news was not meant to be kept behind walls, within the confines of church, or away from the common activities of life and death.

Like the gospel, we were meant to live out there. We have been called to be in the world, but not of the world. We are supposed to be light in darkness, hope in the hopeless places, love in the hateful places. We are supposed to live as Christ lived, without a home, elbows-deep in His creation.

Christ came for the sick, not those who thought and continue to think themselves well. He came for those willing to die daily and carry their cross, not those who would hold on to their lives.

Many of us are not overwhelmed by need. We may not live in neighborhoods blighted by social ills. Others of us might live deep in it. Either way, we must seek out need in order to meet it in Christ's name. We have to pursue the needy. Embracing this call will force us into the world that Christ instructs us to engage.

WE REALIZE THAT LOVE REQUIRES ACTION

Christ's love had substance. From His compassion for the sick, to His redress of the prideful, to His work on the cross, Christ's love acted. When Christ taught about love, He stressed the verb—an imperative. He called for action.

We are tempted at times to think that love is an emotion—empathy for those in need—but it is not. Love is carving off bits of yourself and handing them to someone who has no power to repay. Love is having no ledgers, no sense of self, no desire for glory. Love is taking one step more than you think you can, because the person you are serving can't take steps toward you.

The Good Samaritan loved like this. He did something of substance. He didn't pass by like the others. He had compassion that led him to do something. No qualifications, excuses, or expectations of anything in return. He served the man personally and financially—a man who most of his fellow Samaritans would have avoided because of his race, faith, and lifestyle.[5]

Make no mistake—Christ commands you to do the same. It is not an option. If you are loving your neighbor then you are acting—not just praying, thinking, hoping, worrying, or otherwise. You are acting.

WE FIND TRUE FULFILLMENT AND MEANING AS CHRISTIANS

I have been a Christian almost my entire life. I don't have a radical salvation story, but I do have a radical story of learning to follow Christ. Throughout most of my teen and adult life I have searched for fulfillment as a Christian. At times this has led to worldly success and complete spiritual depression. At other times I have experienced phenomenal spiritual joy in the face of daunting secular concerns. I could find no rhyme or reason to my search. More than anything in life, I wanted to find fulfillment and meaning in what I was doing.

Somewhere along the line I began to think in terms of last-breath equality. I began to evaluate what I was doing with my time and talents based on whether it would have any impact after that last breath. Through this process I gained a pretty remarkable insight.

The things I was doing that had no impact on eternity brought me little, if any, lasting fulfillment. The joy they produced slipped through my fingers. But the things I was doing that had the potential to survive did. Many of my choices and activities stayed the same, but it radically changed my perspective and expectations.

The things I do that touch eternity—sharing my faith, investing in my family, loving my wife, serving my children, giving money and time to humanitarian work that is rooted in the gospel, these things bring me fulfillment.

Everything I do that doesn't have any possible eternal connection brings me nothing lasting. It doesn't mean I don't do them, because many of my responsibilities have to be attended to even though they don't impact eternity. It just means that I don't expect to get fulfillment from them.

In much the same way, when our humanitarian endeavors are not tied to eternity, they won't bring fulfillment. There is an emptiness in all that is "good," but not "eternally good."

Imagine what the world would look like if our work for humanity was always the kind that lasts, the kind that leads to eternal fulfillment and life, both for us and those we're seeking to help.

Every day I die again, and again I'm reborn

Every day I have to find the courage

To walk out into the street

With arms out

—U2, "BREATHE"

Chapter 6

GO FORTH
AND CONQUER

I once had a math professor who ended each class with the words, "Go forth and conquer." It seemed to have little application to math class, but it did always make me feel good and it brings to mind the simple truth that at some point, after considering all of the ideas contained in this book and the interviews that follow—you simply have to set a course and go at it with gusto.

We live in a broken world filled with broken people—people who are wasting away emotionally, physically, and spiritually, and have a thirst that cannot be quenched by human hands. This is the world into which Christ was born and into which He commands us to go, to walk, to touch, and to love in His name and in submission to His plan. Humanity and God's creation is wasting away under the weight of sin, and only Christ holds the "words of eternal life," so where else would we go?[1]

Of this we can be certain: a person's eternal destiny is not transformed by a good deed done on their behalf, but by their experiencing a life-altering personal meeting with the risen Christ. Our deeds have only the power to impact physical lives if they are not done in and through the power of Christ. In Him, life, wholeness, and the fullness of the gospel are found. Apart from Him, only shadows and remnants of His glory are experienced.

Just as He did two thousand years ago, Christ is making His appeal for all to come to Him—the weak, weary, and disenfranchised along with the strong and mighty of this earth. He is making His appeal for the blind to receive sight, the hungry to be fed, and the lost to be found. He is making His appeal for whosoever might believe and He seeks to make that appeal through you.

There is no greater calling, no greater mission, no greater work than to carry in us the hope of glory, the presence of the risen Lord, and the words of eternal life. We should carry in our hands food, water, medicine, justice, and relief, in any and every form. But our hearts, minds, and souls must be reserved for Christ alone. The hope of glory is Christ in us, not what we do on His behalf.

Just as the masses left Christ two thousand years ago when His call became difficult, His ways became unpopular, and His perspective became detested, we are being challenged to walk away from Christ's humanitarianism. A humanitarianism that acknowledges that only spiritual, redemptive transformation can lead to true external revitalization and accepts that people die from the inside out.

We can walk away or acknowledge that sin and separation from God are the fundamental causes of sickness, suffering, social injustice, and death, and that while you and I might be able to treat the symptoms of sin, only God holds the cure. We can walk away or accept that all of Christ's humanitarian efforts occurred on His way to the cross.

Biblical humanitarian investment, social Christianity at its purest, does not solve social problems or reveal our goodness; it solves personal temporal problems and in so doing reveals Christ's goodness. As John the Baptist rightly proclaimed, we must decrease in all that we do, and Christ must increase in all that is seen and experienced by those we impact.

What would it look like if the body of Christ was fully committed to His mission, not ours, and fully invested in His earthly passions, not ours? What if we spent our lives the way He spent His? What would it look like if we decreased and He increased?

Perhaps more people would be engaged for the gospel, meeting more spiritual and physical needs, in more places in the world. Perhaps we would spend our days as Christ spent most of His, simply walking amongst humanity, meeting needs and spiritually impacting lives.

Christ healed, fed, loved, and engaged people, all the while knowing that His Father's will was for Him to die on a cross, take a last breath, experience a final heartbeat, and give up His spirit. It is divinely astounding that on the way to the cross, Christ stopped to ask Bartimaeus, a person just like you and me, "What do you want me to do for you?"

What do you—one of my broken, hurting, dying creations—want Me—the Creator of the universe standing before you, sustaining your life, preparing to die for your sins—to do for you?

What would your answer have been? What could you possibly have asked for once you realized the enormity of the question?

We will all partake in a last breath of equality and in that moment we will stand side by side with people whose lives were filled with love and hate, sickness and health, plenty and want, fame and failure. Christ will meet each of us in that moment: the child who died of cancer, the woman who died of starvation, the father who died of AIDS, the rich man who died in his riches, and the poor man who died in perfect health. Christ will meet each of us in that moment—what will He say to you?

If we focus our lives on things that won't survive that last breath, we risk being told by our Savior that we succeeded in feeding, clothing, housing, and physically curing men, women, and children who are spending an eternity separated from Him. We risk being told that in our zeal for solving temporal problems, we forgot that people are eternal.

On the other hand, if we reject the necessity of meeting needs and touching lives, we risk being asked why we ignored the way our Master lived and His call for us to be engaged in His creation. We risk seeing the eyes of the destitute men, women, and children we passed by on our way to church in the eyes of our Master.

We need to remember who the humanitarian Jesus was and emulate

Him. He so loved the world that He came to seek and to save the lost. He was focused on spiritual regeneration, but made temporal investment in His plan of redemption.

Christ invested His life in the temporal needs of the lost, drawing them to Himself, so that they might not just be healed, but also see their true eternal need for Him. If we are correctly following His example, every ounce of our social, humanitarian, and temporal investments will be focused on doing the same.

Go forth and conquer . . .

PART TWO:

the
INTERVIEWS

The people who love, because they are freed through the truth of God, are the most revolutionary people on earth. They are the ones who upset all values; they are the explosives in human society. Such persons are the most dangerous.

—DIETRICH BONHOEFFER[1]

INTRODUCTION

Now you know what we think. You might be starting to know what you think. But what do people who are active in these issues think?

The point of this book is not for you to agree or disagree with us. The point is that you begin to reconsider how you should engage human need in light of your faith and understanding of God's call on your life. Because of this, we have refrained from engaging any specific issue in the first part of this book or to suggest practical ways of handling issues on the ground.

On the one hand, it would be arrogant of us to think that we know how to work out these issues in the everyday affairs of those active in serving the needs of people around the globe. How you work out these issues will depend on where you are in the world, what you are doing, and how you believe God is calling you.

On the other hand, we are convinced that if you begin to ask the right questions and have the foundation for answering them in accordance with Scripture, the answers you arrive at and how they impact your actions will be directed by Christ.

Consider Paul in Athens, in Acts 17, walking around the greatest city on earth at that time observing the culture, thinking, and everyday life of the Greeks. His point of view was unique because unlike most people who would have focused on the beauty of the art and culture, or the needs of the people in the marketplace, or the opportunities for business, Paul was greatly distressed; his spirit was provoked and grieved.

Paul saw the worship of idols and the absence of reconciliation with God. He may have seen other issues and needs, but his point of view led him to begin reasoning with the people of Athens as an ambassador of Christ so that they might meet the true God and be reconciled to Him.

How Paul saw the world and what he thought influenced what he did. He could have done many good things in Athens that would have served the Lord. He could have started a church, set up a mission, provided for the poor, fed the hungry, or healed the sick. These things would have been good. But Paul, because of the way he looked at the world, didn't do those things. He went to the synagogue and marketplace and reasoned with the people who happened to be there.

The question isn't whether you look at the world the way Paul did, but rather, whether you look that the world the way God desires for you.

Each of the people we have included in this section of the book, and others we didn't have room for, are trying to look at the world and react the way God is leading them. The point of the interviews isn't to critique, but rather to gain insight from how each of the individuals and organizations is working out God's call to invest in His creation and serve His desires.

We hope you enjoy the stories that are included and that they ignite a desire in you to find your place of engagement in God's work of investment in, and redemption of, His creation.

GUIDE TO INTERVIEWS

Name	Organization	Area	Page
Ron Sider	Evangelicals for Social Action	Social Justice and the Social Gospel	85
David Batstone	Not For Sale	Global Slavery and Justice	95
Mark Batterson	National Community Church Washington, D. C.	Social Investment and the Church	103
Tony Campolo	Evangelical Association for the Promotion of Education	Social Justice	111
Jerry Wiles	Living Water International	Water	119
Jim Moriarty	Surfrider Foundation	The Environment	127
Gilbert Lennox	Glenabbey Church of Belfast	Peace and Reconciliation	135
Franklin Graham	Samaritan's Purse	Global Humanitarian Aid	143
Gary Haugen	International Justice Mission	Global Slavery and Justice	155
Rusty Pritchard	Flourish	Environment	165
Francis Chan	Cornerstone Church, Simi Valley, CA	Social Investment and the Church	173
Brad Corrigan	Love Light & Melody	Poverty	183
Isaac Shaw	Delhi Bible Institute	Poverty and the Church in India	191
Bryan Kemper	Stand True Ministries	Abortion	199
Mike Yankoski	The Ranch	Homelessness	207

1

RON **SIDER**

President, Evangelicals for Social Action

Author of *Rich Christians in an Age of Hunger; The Scandal of Evangelical Politics; I Am Not a Social Activist; Good News and Good Works*

Ron Sider wrote the book on this topic. He actually has written many books on this topic, but *Rich Christians in an Age of Hunger* impacted a generation the way Sheldon's *In His Steps* and Rauschenbusch's *Christianity and the Social Crisis* had done before. Since the inception of the Evangelicals for Social Action in 1973, and surely before that, Sider has existed as a lightning rod of debate and attack, from both the left and right. While complex in application, Sider's goal is quite simple: a church where both evangelism and social action work in harmony. Our discussion was both an honor for me and a test of my mental acuity.

Christian Buckley: You made a statement in one of your books that "I'm not a social activist." It was the title of the book and the title of a chapter. What is the difference between a social activist and a socially active disciple of Jesus Christ?

Ron Sider: I think the key is, "Is Jesus the center?" My point in that chapter is, I'm not committed first of all to peace or justice or any other issue, I'm committed to Jesus. I'm committed to the Scriptures. And it seems to me that Jesus calls me to be a peacemaker and to care about the poor, but it's very easy even for an evangelical social activist to get so focused on the social action that we neglect Jesus as the center or neglect evangelism. I felt called way back by the end of grad school to be an evangelical social activist, but I vowed I would not be a part of, to the extent that I could shape it, a renewal of the old social gospel (where we had a weak theology and lost evangelism). I said I wanted to be focused on Jesus. I want the Bible to be the center of our authority. I want to maintain an orthodox theology and a passion for evangelism.

CB: Going back to the 1970s, a lot happened. Your drafting of the Chicago Declaration, the launch of ESA, the meetings and covenant that came out of Lausanne. What was the experience of that?

RS: In the '30s and '40s, fundamentalism basically withdrew and wasn't substantially engaged with seeking to change society. Beginning with Carl Henry and his "Uneasy Conscience" in '47, there was a new group of evangelicals that were saying, "We have to engage the world. We have to be intellectually engaged, we have to be engaged in science, we have to be engaged in culture, we have to be politically engaged." They began to develop a more holistic approach to what evangelicalism should be. That certainly developed slowly, and by the early '70s you had a new group of young evangelicals who were really impatient with what we read as a lack of social concern generally in the evangelical world. So I organized the meeting in Chicago, and we invited about forty evangelical leaders. It included young evangelicals and older evangelicals. And what came of it was a new vigorous call for evangelicals on the basis of a solid theology to be socially engaged.

CB: What was the response to that call?

RS: I would say beginning in the late '60s, '70s, when I got started, the standard view of evangelical leaders was what Billy Graham said at the Lausanne Congress on World Evangelization—evangelism is the primary mission of the church and if you've got a little time and money left over you can do a little bit of social action. What happened in the Lausanne Covenant Section 5 was very crucial. It was because of Stott, Samuel Escobar, René Padilla, and other younger evangelicals that Section 5 was included. It said that evangelism and social action are not the same thing, but they are both part of our Christian responsibility. That section played a key role in a long debate over several decades. Today, virtually any evangelical leader you ask would agree that biblical Christians are supposed to do both evangelism and social ministry. Exactly what the shape of the social ministry should be is debated, but we're supposed to do both. Over the last four decades, there's been a growing evangelical concern for social ministry. There are dozens and dozens of big relief agencies. Never before in my life has the most prominent evangelical voice in this country been talking about the poor the way Rick Warren is. God's concern for the poor has become more and more important to evangelicals.

CB: How should the average Christian who thinks about these issues engage the idea of doing both? Aren't we drawn to one or the other? Don't we see polarity in groups who advocate for either the gospel or the social investment part of the equation?

RS: Let me say one preliminary thing, and I think it's absolutely key. As an evangelical, I'm committed to orthodox theology. I'm committed to the Bible as the final authority. That's my starting point and absolute standard.

One of the most crucial questions is, "What is the gospel?" I've got a whole book on this—*Good News and Good Works*. I think there has been a kind of unbiblical Platonism that has been profoundly a part of Christian faith in a whole variety of ways. Evangelicalism reflects that Platonism when we say that the gospel or evangelism is "saving souls." Persons are not just souls. They're body-soul unities. They are whole persons, and if you only talk about saving souls, you're falling into a sort of Platonic misunderstanding of what the Bible is about.

A lot of evangelicalism thinks the core of the gospel is forgiveness of sins. What really matters is that your sins are forgiven so that you can go to heaven when you die. I want to say that's flatly unbiblical. It's not because it's untrue. It's a crucial part of the gospel, but for Jesus, the gospel is the good news of the kingdom.

What Jesus does is say, My Messianic kingdom begins within history, and in this time between My first coming and second coming, the kingdom is growing, it's becoming more visible in the church. But it's not yet complete, and sin and evil will continue until I return at the second coming, when finally, I'll complete the victory. And once you understand that the gospel is the good news of the kingdom, then you can't say that it's just forgiveness of sins. And it's not just preparing us for eternity. The goal of what we're waiting for is Christ's returning at some time in the future and His completing the victory over all sin and evil. This good earth which sin has messed up so badly at every level (in personal lives, in our social structures) will be made whole. Christ will complete the victory over sin, and we will live with the risen Christ in this transformed earth.

So when I talk about evangelism, I mean inviting people who are not now Christians to accept Jesus Christ as their personal Lord and Savior and to accept His gospel. But that gospel is not just the forgiveness of sins so you can go to heaven; it is also the good news that His kingdom is breaking in.

CB: One of the things that strikes me is that whoever it is that I'm engaging with, whether they're sick, poor, rich, or whatever—that individual has both a temporal existence and physicality, and an eternal existence. Christ was fixated on both the temporal and the eternal. When I look at Christianity today, sometimes I wonder where we are in that spectrum of focus.

RS: I understand the point you're making now very well, and I agree with you. There's a powerful materialism in American culture that's unbiblical because Jesus said that it's better to lose the whole world . . . than to lose one's relationship with the living God. What biblical faith does is affirm the goodness of the material world, although it's been messed up by sin, it's still very good. But it's not everything. In fact, it is not even as important as [the idea] that I'm going to have a relationship with God forever. And so we must hold those in balance. I think biblical balance is one of the absolutely crucial things. Our acceptance with God is absolutely important, and I say regularly that I'd rather lose everything I have in the material world than lose my relationship with God.

So there's this general materialism in American culture and I think a lot of evangelicals have really bought into it in a very deep way without admitting it explicitly, and then at the same time, they have this kind of Platonic spiritualism where the main thing is getting saved so that you go to heaven when you die because your soul is saved. In both cases (the materialism and the truncated view of the gospel), the problem is being unbiblical.

CB: I think we still have people who say, "Let's just preach the gospel," and people who say, "Let's not focus on the gospel, let's focus on what Jesus would do." In both areas my question isn't so much what He did, but why He did it. Is that fair?

RS: My answer is precisely in the understanding of the gospel. He did both because the gospel is the wholeness of the Messianic kingdom breaking into history. Sinful people have to be forgiven or they can't be accepted by our holy God. The forgiveness part is central to Jesus. He tells parable after parable about God longing to forgive prodigal sons and daughters. There's no question about that. But then He spends equal amounts of time healing sick bodies, and that makes sense within a gospel of the kingdom. It doesn't make sense if the gospel is only forgiveness of sins. At best, if the gospel is just the forgiveness of sins, the only reason you do social action is a kind of bait.

I think it's certainly the case that if a person only has physical well-being, and never learns about Jesus Christ and never embraces Christ and is therefore not on the way to living forever with Him, then we don't have a good outcome. But I think there's also a sense in which it's important to say that social action is a good in itself, although it's by no means the whole good that whole people need. Whole people need to know Jesus and they need to have decent health care, enough food, etc. There's a valid theological basis for working at having people out of poverty and having health care, and having a decent environment, but I don't think for a minute that's all they need for well-being. They need a living relationship with God who made them.

CB: I have this fear that Christianity has gotten wrapped up in issues. The pendulum seems to swing between the "conservative position" against homosexuality, abortion, pornography, etc., and "liberal" issues like poverty and AIDS. It seems to me that Christ kind of said, "Let the issues be the issues. I'm not trying to cure poverty here, I'm dealing with people who are hungry or poor or blind."

RS: One part of my criticism of evangelical political engagement in the last twenty-five years is that it hasn't been biblical enough. I'm conservative on sexuality and marriage and abortion and I'm opposed to gay marriage. But I'm also concerned with justice for the poor and peacemaking. We've been too narrowly focused on one or two issues. Now the thing I don't want to do is swing the other way and forget about sexuality and marriage and pornography and just focus on justice, peace, and creation care. Biblical balance is crucial.

But the deeper question that you were getting at is when you say Jesus was concerned about persons, not issues. Persons are what matter, but systems shape persons in profound ways. The structures and systems matter, but they're not all-important. We care about the systems because we care about persons.

One thing that frustrates me is that we have got conservatives talking almost exclusively about the fact that bad personal decisions create poverty. And we have liberals focused on the way bad systems contribute to poverty. I've lived among the poor, and it is clear that part of it is bad choices and it's just silly not to admit that. And to solve that you have to have conversion and lead people to Christ so people make different decisions because the Holy Spirit has transformed them. But part of it is that the systems aren't fair. If the gospel is the good news of the kingdom, then I think Jesus is saying not just that He cares about individuals, but He's also creating the new Israel. He calls twelve disciples. It's a conscious reference to the twelve tribes and He is wanting a new social order, which inevitably has structure.

People are sinners at the center of their beings, and so our problems are deeper than the social structures, but social structures make things worse.

CB: There is a finality to how we look at these issues. And I think that's the difficulty of the average Christian who picks this up and says, "I love these ideas, I love to wrestle with these ideas, but there's a kid in the village in Africa who is going to die in the next hour. What am I supposed to do about that?" Or, "There's a kid fifteen miles down the road who's being oppressed in poverty. He only has so much time." That's where I want to push people to think.

RS: That is the question. When you realize that urgency, do you then spend more of your time on inviting people to Christ or more of your time on meeting social need?

CB: At that fulcrum point, one person may say, "I'm more interested in salvation than social issues," and one person may be the other way around. These are not just semantics because your view is going to impact the interaction you have and the allocation of your time and resources.

RS: I think it's crucial. I think that it's very proper theologically to focus on the fact that we have few years here and time is short and people are dying without Christ. But they are also dying in poverty, and that's unnecessary. So there's an urgency in that people wouldn't have to be hungry if we acted, and there's an urgency about people learning about Christ.

Jesus has to be the norm. Anybody who basically says or practices the claim that we're supposed to spend most of our time and energy on social action and that evangelism is not very important, or the other way, is just not being faithful to Jesus. It seems to me that as a community, we're supposed to be doing a lot of both. My way of saying it is, when it comes to money, time, and resources, I want the church to spend roughly the same amount of time on evangelism and social action.

Some of my friends want to say that social action is evangelism, and I say no. It can lead to evangelism, it can open doors for evangelism, it can protect evangelism, but evangelism is not the same thing as social action.

I just think, bottom-line, if Jesus is our Lord, then He has to be our example theologically. We've got to do both, but they're not the same thing. I could have worked for decades to try to end apartheid in South Africa, but it wouldn't have been the same thing as inviting a Jewish student I met there to accept Jesus. Both things are good, but they're not identical. It is also true that it was precisely because he knew that I cared about justice that he was able to hear the invitation in a new way.

DAVID **BATSTONE**

President and Founder, Not For Sale

Author of *Not for Sale; Saving the Corporate Soul*

David Batstone, founder and president of the Not For Sale campaign, is a professor of ethics at the University of San Francisco and worked with Jim Wallis for six years as executive editor of *Sojourners* magazine. At Not For Sale, he wants to equip and mobilize "smart activists to deploy innovative solutions to re-abolish slavery in their own backyards and across the globe." It's not a "Christian" organization, but that isn't what matters to him. He loves Christ and wants you to care about the enslaved.

Christian Buckley: How do you define slavery?

David Batstone: I define slavery very much in line with the Thirteenth Amendment of the U.S. Constitution, the notion of involuntary servitude. It's not low wages, it's not poor environmental conditions; it's forcing someone to do labor against their will for someone else's profit. Really, it parallels directly the situation of the children of Israel in Egypt. God hears their cries and raises up Moses and Aaron to be their redeemers.

CB: So it is a "Christian" issue, not just a social issue.

DB: The root of true redemption is directly related to slavery. It is to free from whatever binds. Physical slavery really takes away the freedom that God has given each of us. Jesus never says, "I've come here simply to redeem your spirit," but rather, "I've come to redeem you as one who has been created in the image of God." For many of us who live in North America, it is spiritual bondage that we face and we need to be redeemed from those things that oppress us and those things that keep us from being the people that God wants us to be; but there are large numbers of populations around the globe that are not only in search of spiritual liberation, but also physical liberation that's taken away their God-given destiny.

CB: I don't know what the statistic is now, but there are about twenty-seven million slaves in the world. In the face of a number like that, it seems there's sort of a collective reticence to acknowledge the breadth of the problem. Why do you think that is?

DB: Well, you know, there's almost a sense where we look to see if there's anything that could be done by changing a law or by pouring money on the problem, in order to to change it. I think slavery is a complex or sophisticated crime or crisis because there are small ma-and-pa traffickers and there are mafia traffickers. In a place like the Philippines, there's a high percentage of law enforcement officers who are profiting from the trafficking of human beings. It has been historically hard to do more than just bring awareness, but it really behooves anyone who wants to bring about change to not simply feel that if you could only make people feel bad about a situation, if only people were aware, somehow something magically happens. The next step is to create tangible handles and bridges that get people to assess that their action actually matters, and it starts to mitigate the problem. That is what we are trying to do.

CB: How has Christianity reacted to the problem in terms of, on the one hand, local churches, and on the other hand, institutionalized Christianity?

DB: When we launched, this stuff wasn't visible to many Americans—particularly traffic happening inside the United States. For that reason, a lot of our work really needed to be poured into making it real enough so you could see this is something that starts in your backyard and goes to the other side of the world.

And so, there's a great opportunity for the church to say, Our identity, who we are at our base, our foundation, is to be about redemption of all God's children. That's how we fought slavery at the time of the African slave trade, through abolitionist churches, and that's why today we can lead on this. And I've been gratified over the last two-and-a-half years to see that it has been people of faith who are leading in this. They really have become invested whether it's creating shelters for the victims, working hand in hand with law enforcement to shut down traffickers, or change laws.

CB: In your mission statement you use the term "smart activists." What is a smart activist?

DB: It's someone who takes strategic action and then based on the results learns how to improve that action so that it can be even more effective. We concluded that so much advocacy and action is kind of knee-jerk, soft, uninformed, and therefore reaps dismal results. We have really focused on everything that we do to say, How do we equip those who want to join in this action so that they become even more skilled in what they're doing?

CB: Do you get criticism because Not For Sale is not a "Christian" nonprofit? What went into your thinking as a follower of Christ in terms of the difference between a Christian nonprofit and simply a nonprofit?

DB: For me—and those who started Not for Sale with me—it was just more of a personal approach as to how we wanted to bring compassion and justice. We said, If we seriously want to end this, we can't ghettoize it as just a Christian activity. We wanted to be able to link with public schools, secular universities, corporations, and governments, in addition to people of faith. And so we set out to start an organization that had a mission that was very clear—to provide freedom for those who are in captivity—without narrowing it to a creed.

At the same time, we articulated very clearly that we wanted to create an environment for the organization where people did not have to leave their beliefs at the door. We have a Freedom Sunday where we create sermon resources, hymns, Bible study guides, without any kind of sense of shame or awkwardness around that. At the same time, there is a Jewish synagogue movement in Not For Sale, there are groups of university students at state secular universities. I think it's healthy that they see that we need each other. We can stand together in an advocacy base in Washington, D.C., and call for the same kind of compassion and justice, even though we may not see eye to eye on what got us into the seat next to each other. That was a personal reason.

What I didn't really anticipate was that it would be almost an invisible watershed in terms of where the Christian church sees its own self-identity right now. There will be some pastors and churches who say the reason we want to be involved with NFS [Not For Sale] is that you don't use the adjective *Christian* in front of your organization. That's how we want to reach our community. At the same time, we have other churches who say, "We love what NFS does, we love your activities, what you accomplish, but we have written in our by-laws that we will not support any organization that's not Christian." I'll push them: What do you mean by "not Christian"? I'm a follower of Jesus, I'm on staff, this is why we do what we do. And the response is, "Yeah, but that's not your label or creed."

CB: There are people who would say, "You know, it's great that NFS is doing what you do, but if you're not 'sharing the gospel,' then you're not doing the right thing." How would you respond to that criticism?

DB: Our job is to free people to be able to make choices that will determine their destiny. After they have that freedom, I think there are other parts of the body of Christ that can step in. We acknowledge that there's more that can put you into bondage than simply the chains around your ankles, and so the process of redemption is a holistic one. A great example of that is, we have a terrific partnership with YWAM (Youth With A Mission) International, and they don't want to become an abolitionist organization per se, and we don't want to be a church-planting organization, but in their church planting around the globe, they are finding people who are trafficked or are in captivity, in slavery, not able to stay in any kind of community or body of Christ. They work with us, helping to identify and do what our mission is really targeted to. In turn, in freeing them, what a wonderful thing for people to be able to seek God with other people in community.

But we do get the question. I went to the National Prayer Breakfast (NPB) this year and I was asked to speak as part of the workshops that surround the NPB, and before I spoke, there were several speakers, and they talked about the importance of prayer and how tempting it is to betray your spiritual values, and focused on spiritual growth and spiritual life and integrity. All of which is incredibly important in Washington, D.C. What I found interesting, when I got up to speak about my work, why I do NFS, and I spoke about what our aim is—when I finished, hands went up, and they said, "I didn't hear you say anything about the spiritual side."

I answered them straight out—the first couple. And then I said, "What's really fascinating to me is, I've been listening to the other speeches today, and no one in this audience raised a hand to the previous three speakers and said, 'You talked about the spiritual life, but are you really helping people—those whose lives are devastated by poverty or slavery or by other forms of oppression?' No one asked why they may not be looking at a holistic gospel, but you're concerned immediately, when I talked about the fact of justice, that somehow I had a skewed gospel." What is our fear? What is our bias in terms of how we understand holistic ministry? Why do we as Christians tend to be immediately suspect of anyone who talks about justice when we don't share that sense of bias when we focus on spiritual gifts?

CB: It seems there's a misunderstanding of how very important basics like water, freedom, food, and clothing are. Most of the world is struggling with issues that we never even come across. Do you have a sense that these things get minimalized? When someone says, "It's great that you're doing this, but what are you doing on the spiritual side?"—is that a minimization of just how bad it really is?

My reaction would be, "How are you going to share the gospel with someone who is enslaved in a brothel? How is that going to work, to walk in and say, 'I realize that you're a sex slave, but I want to talk to you about the love of Jesus Christ,' without doing anything about that plight?"

DB: I've concluded that it's really hard for us to pursue spiritual growth until we're willing to follow Jesus on the road to discipleship, because we'll read the Scripture, and we'll pray and ask questions of God based on where our feet are planted, what our experiences are. If I stay rooted in my level, if everybody that goes to church looks like me, lives like me, and smells like me, then probably I'm not going to be moved to ask new questions like, I wonder what the gospel says when you can't have any clean water to drink? How would I read the Bible differently if I was reading it on an empty stomach? How would I pray with others when I'm enslaved and kept away from anyone else because there's danger in us striving for our freedom?

I would read the Bible differently, I would pray differently, and I would certainly have a different perception and approach to my faith if I was in those kinds of dire circumstances. It isn't that you can't grow spiritually if you're not enslaved, impoverished, or starving. It's through our empathy with those who are in those situations that you see Jesus in ministry. If we're not studying Scripture looking for wisdom while also continually taking risks in our discipleship, then we're going to have a truncated spiritual life. I think we should start doing theology at sundown rather than at sunrise. We need to think about what we've learned about God after we look at the course of our day rather than saying, "Everything I know about God will be the same no matter how I live today." That's not minimizing God's absolute nature, it's trying to change our perceived absolute understanding of God's nature and character.

CB: Do we have a need to put more skin in the game as Christians? I get this sense sometimes when we look at these issues that they become cerebral, they become theological, rather than real, life-changing realities for us.

DB: I recently gave the commencement address at a Christian college and challenged the students to realize that there was not a better time to graduate than right now because the world has so much need. This should be the time that the church says, "This is our moment." The world is out of answers right now— economically, politically, socially, culturally. It's looking for answers. We need to be willing to sacrifice ourselves, understand that God so loved the world, and commit to living that love.

Unfortunately, I find my students and those people who are in my community who know I'm a Christian don't reject it based on the authenticity of our practice, but on their misinterpretations of our beliefs.

CB: What is the solution to that problem?

DB: I think this generation is calling for authentic discipleship. We should lead with that and then be able to articulate and express why we follow that path even though we stumble—why we continue to follow that. We've been forgiven to be free, and in that freedom we pursue a life of service and giving even unto the cross.

3

MARK **BATTERSON**

Pastor, National Community Church in Washington, D.C.

Author of Primal; Wild Goose Chase; In a Pit with a Lion

Mark Batterson founded and pastors National Community Church (NCC) in Washington, D.C. It meets in theaters across the city, operates a coffee house called Ebenezers (which happens to be next to the old row home that houses the church offices), and close to 70 percent of the congregation is twentysomething D.C. singles—almost half of which are new attendees every year. Safe to say, this is not your typical church. Mark's daily blogs are read by thousands more than attend the church and he sits within a block of Union Station, the SEC, and the Federal Courts building. From that vantage point it is also safe to say that he might have a unique perspective on what is going on in the hearts and minds of Christians traditionally interested in social issues. But NCC is not a cause-driven church—and it stays that way on purpose.

Christian Buckley: You're doing ministry in a place where American Christian political thought has transitioned over the years. Have you been impacted by that?

Mark Batterson: I think that in a sense, "Christianity" is incarnated and reincarnated in every generation and every culture and it looks different at different times and in different places. Part of that is a testament to the "omni- relevance" of who God is and His ability to relate to His creation in every form and fashion. Some of that is determined by the spirit of the times. Most recently, I think our big problem has been that we're more known for what we're against than for what we're for. We have tended to focus on sins of commission—*don't do this, don't do that*—but we ignore sins of omission—what you would have, could have, and should have done. I'm kind of talking out of what I wrote in this next book [*Primal*], that we've got to be great in the Great Commandment—love God with all your heart, soul, mind, and strength—and we've got to be more known for what we're for.

I do see a shift toward, at least in the 70 percent single twenty-somethings I pastor, a cause orientation. It's not unique to this generation. I think everybody rallies around causes, but whether it's the environment or social justice issues, people need a cause to rally around, and for a long time, the churches ignored that.

CB: I'm guessing your congregation has a big worldview. With the generation you're working with, there's no disconnect between me, someone in Europe, and someone in Africa. How is that impacting their view of the gospel? Are they looking at the world differently and therefore coming to their faith differently because of that?

MB: Yeah. We're trying to push the issue. This year a major initiative for us was called our A1:8 Initiative—Acts 1:8—"you'll receive power and you'll be my witnesses in Jerusalem, Judea, Samaria and the ends of the earth." The way we practically tried to put that verse into practice was doing ten missions trips to ten countries this past year. I feel that one mission trip is worth fifty-two sermons. You have to get people out of their environment and into another environment where they can be exposed to true needs before they can put their "needs" in perspective. We did everything from a trip to Thailand working with a ministry called "The Well" that is helping to rescue women from the sex trade there, to a ministry center outside of Addis in

Ethiopia that is reaching out to an AIDS colony. We tried to latch on to some different causes that we felt could really rally people. We're trying to really push that envelope and help our people think in more global terms.

I think the generation that we're reaching does that more naturally because it's the Google effect, the world's so small. More and more people are spending a semester abroad or working globally. At NCC, the categories that we think about in church are the people who attend one of our five locations —we think of them as immediate family, and the people who listen by a webcast or podcast—and that's thousands of people every week—in our national and global extended family.

CB: I read an interview where you said that you had been rethinking the idea of missions. How so?

MB: We think we're doing good to get people to invest a week of their life going on a short-term trip. That is good. But we're thinking about launching a café ministry in Berlin, and I love the possibility of challenging people to give a year of their lives. Most of the relocation decisions in life have to do with occupation. Why can't they have something to do with the kingdom? Why can't you relocate because of kingdom reasons, not just occupational reasons? Ebenezers Coffeehouse is another good example. We want to be giving a million dollars to missions. As a church, we'll give more than half a million dollars to missions this year, and we will continue to grow that, and the day will come when we're giving a million dollars. Every penny of profit from Ebenezers goes to missions, or local outreach. We netted about one hundred thousand dollars last year. Every penny goes to those causes. If we had a chain of ten coffee houses netting that amount, then you have a million dollars for missions.

CB: One of things I love about NCC and your passion is your focus on the concept of the marketplace. It's everywhere at NCC. Church isn't church if it's not out there. Where did that come from?

MB: When I felt called into ministry, into pastoring a church, my greatest fear was that I would get quarantined behind the four walls of a church building and lose touch with people who are far away from God. You see too many churches that have become inward-focused and exist for the people who are already there. I feel we needed to exist for the person who isn't here yet. We want to go after people who are unchurched. My goal is to get people to the cross—if people get to the cross and they're offended by the cross, I can't do anything about that. The problem is that most of us offend people before they get to the cross. We have these cultural loopholes that people have to jump through before they even hear the message. We wanted to be in a marketplace environment and remove every barrier. When we started meeting in the movie theaters at Union Station, I realized that twenty-five million people pass through there and the theater was a safe environment sociologically. People knew how to get there.

The vision behind Ebenezers was an extrapolation of that. Jesus didn't just hang out at the synagogue, He hung out at wells. Wells were these natural gathering places in ancient culture. Coffeehouses are postmodern wells. With great intentionality we wanted to create a place where the church and community can cross paths. Every day hundreds of customers come through there and we are rubbing shoulders with them.

CB: How has your congregation—the age and turnover reality—impacted the way you look at doing ministry?

MB: There's a sense of urgency. This summer we had several hundred interns that were here for six to ten weeks and then gone. It's the nature of the beast in D.C. With the podcast/webcast/blog we maintain some connection points, so it really is that immediate family, extended family. It is a highly educated and driven group. People who come to work on the Hill come because they want to make a difference. I respect that. Whether I agree with their politics or not, we're an incredibly diverse congregation politically because we made the decision with great intentionality to be a-political. I saw too many churches that use the pulpit as a platform for public policy. We're not afraid to talk about issues that we need to talk about, but we're very careful not to align ourselves with a political party or political personalities.

CB: Have you seen those political influences in your people?

MB: We've created an environment where we're split right down the middle and have a free-market system of small groups where we allow our leaders to get a vision from God and go for it. It's not top down. We don't tell them what to do. Over the years, a lot of what could be called social justice groups have come to life. Those groups revolve around issues that they care deeply about. Not every group has seen eye-to-eye on every issue with our groups. That's where it gets tricky, because if something is unbiblical—against the principles of Scripture—then we need to establish a boundary; but if something is "a-biblical"—just beyond Scripture, but not contradictory—that's where you need latitude. That's territory where most churches don't want to go. It's easier to draw simple boundaries instead of wrestling with issues intellectually and spiritually.

CB: How have you seen things break down or go well with respect to the issue groups?

MB: My first thought is that on a grand level, we want to help our people identify their passions—what makes them mad, sad, or smile. When we do that, we want to release them to pursue those passions. With our ten missions trips, we asked the congregation, "What do you have a burden for?" Many of the trips came out of those passions. From my pastoral perspective, it's about helping people identify their passions and finding ways to pursue them.

CB: It sounds like everything you're doing from the pulpit and knowledge perspective has to get down to the integration level. If it's not integrated with your work, where you live, with your passion, then something's gone wrong. If it's only about coming and learning, then the notion of church for you is a failure.

MB: Almost everybody I know is educated beyond their level of obedience. There are some people who need to know more, and we need to study the Word and be in the Word, but it's about us taking those simple principles and living them out. You cannot divide the good news of the gospel from living it out. I'm a "both-ends" thinker. It's not enough to know the truth in an intellectual sense, you have to live it out.

CB: So you are trying to focus your church on living out Christ's example.

MB: Yes, but there is a key distinction for me. Religion is us doing something for God. Christianity in its purest form is what Christ has done for us. Those are two very different things and I think some put the cart before the horse and then it can become this gospel of good works, and that's not the gospel. It's not about what I can do for Him, it's about what He's done for me, and then when you come to the saving knowledge of the truth and you know what He's done for you, it motivates you to live your life for Him. It's not either-or.

CB: How are you personally and as a church defining *evangelism*?

MB: I've thought about it a lot and I have a lot of different definitions. One of my personal definitions is that worship is bragging about God to God and evangelism is bragging about God to others.

To answer more specifically, when we do servant evangelism, the way we describe it is that we're showing the love of Christ in practical ways. I think there's a place for, "How can they believe in Him whom they have not heard?" There's a place for that verbal communication piece, and I don't want to minimize that. It's critical. But I also don't want to minimize that it's about our lives being attractive enough for people to actually want what we have. We try to take the approach of loving people with our lives; let's be known for what we're for, let's make a difference, and at the same time let's preach the Word competently, creatively, courageously. Like Paul said in Thessalonians, "I didn't just share the Word, I shared my life." It's that kind of dual concept. The biggest mistake we've made is we've tried to do evangelism without relationship, and that rarely produces fruit. We've tried to see how we can serve, love, give, and bless, and then tell people why we're doing it and extend the invitation.

CB: We touched on this earlier, but I presume there are a lot of "requests" of you and your church to engage issues. What has your thinking been personally and from your church about engaging issues and causes? How have you resisted that temptation?

MB: A lot of churches try to be all things to all people, but that's not a kingdom mind-set. Every church is on the same team. We just play different roles. If I really appreciate different churches on Capitol Hill or in the D.C. area, it frees me up. We don't have to be all things to all people. We had to draw a line in the sand. We can't get behind every initiative, every cause, even if we agree with and believe in those things. The way we accomplish that is through the free-market system of small groups. We allow them to start a group. "You can give expression to that, we're behind you, we love you, we believe in you. No, we're not going to do a lot of pulpit announcements for you because we can't do that for one hundred groups." Saying yes to one thing is saying no to another.

CB: So, in conclusion, what do you see as your primary role?

MB: We're going to focus on introducing people to Jesus Christ. Help people find that relationship, grow as a disciple, and in the truest sense find that calling, passion, and dream that God has for them. It's a holistic, kingdom effort.

4

TONY **CAMPOLO**

President, Evangelical Association for the Promotion of Education
Author of *Red Letter Christians* and about thirty-four others

If you don't know Tony Campolo, you should want to. Not because you will agree with everything he says, but because you can't disagree with his passion and relentless pursuit of doing things better. When we sat down in an old hall at Eastern University, I didn't expect to leave understanding him completely, but I also didn't expect to leave respecting him as much as I did. It wasn't that I agreed with everything he said, but at thirty-three, I was struck by the intensity and irreverence to ideology and labels that I discovered in a man of seventy-five years who had advised at least one president and countless other leaders and students.

Christian Buckley: As you look at the landscape of American Christianity, is the current political situation changing the dialogue?

Tony Campolo: It's a very mixed bag. There are many good signs and there are many bad signs. It's a question of how you view things. The glass may be half full or half empty, as the old saying goes. I think the economic downturn, contrary to a lot of sociologists, is one of the best things that could have happened to America. A lot of Christian people are upset because they feel the old ways were what Christians were entitled to. It was a lifestyle in which we were 6 percent of the world's population consuming 43 percent of the world's resources. We just couldn't go on as a consumeristic society at the level of consumerism that had marked us over the last forty years, some would say. It was an immoral lifestyle. There was no justification for living with the kind of affluence that had marked our lifestyles as had been the case. In simple language, we were spending about, this is sociological, at least 65 percent of our income on "stuff" that nobody really needed. And while we were buying "stuff" that nobody needed, half the world was trying to survive on less than two dollars a day. That affluent, obscenely consumptive lifestyle has been challenged by the economic recession and I almost see the hand of God in it.

CB: The church has been largely silent on materialism, but traditionally vocal on "conservative" moral issues. Has the downturn changed that?

TC: I think Rick Warren and Bill Hybels have become very, very sensitive to the needs of the poor. While Franklin Graham and I would not be on the same page on a lot of issues, I think more and more, we are moving to the same page. What he's been doing for poor people around the world has been notable and it has to be chalked up to a social consciousness that might not have been quite as evident ten years ago.

On the other hand, I think that the liberal church mentality that understood Christianity as simply a social justice program has also been challenged. Not only is there an economic downturn, but every major denomination is hemorrhaging and losing members at a rate that staggers the imagination. And so, suddenly, they have become very, very cognizant of the need to win people to Jesus Christ on a personal level. Because in the effort to declare the kingdom of God on earth, there has been the rediscovery of the ideas that you can't have a kingdom without kingdom people. You can't transform the world unless you have agents of transformation and evangelism.

CB: So are we moving left or right?

TC: Perhaps both. I think we are recognizing that if Christ is in you, you will be opposed to torture. If Christ is in you, you will raise questions about war. If Christ is in you, you will be environmentally concerned. Christianity is about inviting people into a relationship with Christ and Christ will then make these persons into agents of social change. When Christ comes in, He begins to change your thinking and your feeling and the more Christ-like you become, in this process of being transformed, the more the things that have moved the heart of God will move your heart. That will make you into a radical in terms of social justice issues.

CB: Many have seen you to be very critical of the "religious right" or the conservative movement in Christian politics, including James Dobson. Why are you critical?

TC: I'll tell you where I raise the question with Dobson and the religious right in general on the issue of abortion—[some] abortions are economically driven. I don't see how you can talk about making abortion illegal [without also talking about] the economic issues that are driving people to have abortions. To do the one without the other is unconscionable. Likewise, I think the Democrats are wrong for being pro-choice. So when you go into the voting booth and you're going to pull the lever, you've got a problem. I have a problem. I like the abortion reduction philosophy of the Democrats, I like the pro-life plank of the Republicans.

I listen to a guy like Dobson and I'm saying, "When in the world are our evangelical Republicans going to stand up and yell against their own party?" Thank God at least Dobson did some of this in the last election.

CB: So you are frustrated with your conservative brothers.

TC: I'm saying, at what point will they begin to raise questions about their Republican party? [Supposedly] we needed to have a Republican congress to overcome *Roe v. Wade.* Well, we got one. Well, we need a President; we got one. Well, we need Republican appointees. Six out of the nine Supreme Court justices were appointed by Republican presidents. Question, simple question. Did the Republicans do anything [about *Roe v. Wade*]? They didn't.

CB: How do we deal with the divide between liberal and conservative evangelicals?

TC: I think Dobson's a very good man and he thinks I'm a good guy too— misled, but he sees me as a good Christian brother. Whenever I say something that's out of line, I can expect to get an email from him and in every case that he has sent me an email he was right and I was wrong.

I think that Jim Dobson, even though I don't agree with him, is a very important voice to be heard because at least he wakes us up to the fact that [the initially proposed health care reform] bill does in fact finance abortions and it doesn't have to. Somebody needs to be saying these things. I don't have the voice that he has. We have a host of political issues that we disagree on, but I'm so glad that he's out there saying the things he's saying and that need to be said. I will criticize him just as he criticizes me, but always recognizing that this is a Christian brother who is saying things that need to be said at this particular time in history.

CB: I've heard you say in interviews and in your book *Red Letter Christians* that at the time of judgment, it's not going to be theological questions that we'll be asked, it's going to be questions about what we did with our lives.

TC: Exactly.

CB: When you make that statement, I'm sure you've had people respond, "Well, wait a minute, Tony. Are you saying it's not about what somebody believes? That it's only about what they do?" I don't hear you saying that.

TC: Here's what I'm saying. One becomes a Christian and will be accepted into the kingdom in terms of his or her relationship with Jesus Christ. But once you fall in love with God, you will fall in love with your neighbor. If you're not in love with your neighbor, that's an evidence that you're not in love with God.

I would say categorically you can only be saved by having a personal relationship with Christ. And one evidence of whether you have a personal relationship with Christ is whether or not you have a personal relationship with the poor and the oppressed.

CB: I'm finding that there is a spectrum in Christianity, and on one end of the spectrum you have people who are entirely focused on the first half of that statement, and on the other half of the spectrum, you have people who are entirely focused on the other part of that statement. Neither is an accurate view of Christianity. Christianity is the two integrated, and I think that's what you're saying.

TC: The kingdom of God is transformed people in a transformed world. If you are trying to transform the world without transforming people, do you have a kingdom? The answer is no. You can't create the kingdom of God without transformed people. Consequently, to talk about any kind of declaration of the kingdom that doesn't make evangelism paramount, is a distortion of the way in which Christ would go about it. How did Christ go about it? Did He go about saying, "Well, I've got to put together a social/political agenda that will challenge the Roman Empire." Not at all. He was creating disciples, people who believed in Him and adopted a lifestyle. And the outcome of that was the transformation of the Roman Empire. And that's where I think we all have to be.

CB: Where do you see the results of this type of thinking?

TC: People who are social-gospel oriented in the liberal mainstream of mainline denominations are more and more shifting over in the direction of evangelism and seeing that if they don't get on this, there's not going to be any social gospel at all because it's people who have been touched by the gospel who become agents of social transformation. On the other hand, I see Franklin Graham moving more and more to this side. He [seems] willing to say, "Even if it's a Muslim country and they are not going to let me preach the gospel, I will still go in there and feed the hungry, and clothe the naked, because this is a way of declaring something about the Christ that I love." So I see a coming together of the left and the right.

CB: That raises a really practical question. One of the challenges that people have and I think have always had in dealing with these two ideas is the reality that while both are true, how they work out practically on the ground and in your life is far more complex. Have you experienced that?

TC: People have to work this stuff out. Ultimately for me it reduced itself down to a book I read when I was fifteen years old: *In His Steps* by Sheldon. The pressing question is, "What would Jesus do?" If Jesus was in your place, what would He do? Isn't that what it means to be a follower of Jesus? So the question is—here's health care. Big issue right now. If Jesus looked at forty-four million Americans, thirteen million hungry children without any health coverage whatsoever, would He be indifferent?

CB: What would you want the average Christian person who might pick this book up to know about you that they probably don't know?

TC: To me, being Christian is being filled with the Holy Spirit. I contend this about social justice, about politics, about economics, about anything: "Unless the Lord builds the house, they labor in vain that build it." That I want first and foremost to be filled with the Holy Spirit. This takes nothing away, as I have already said, from being intensely committed to social justice, intensely committed to the poor and oppressed, intensely opposed to the war in Iraq, intensely proenvironment, intensely all these things. I'm passionate, but I feel the Holy Spirit guiding me and creating within me these intensive concerns about things like the environment, racism, sexism, and of course the one that I get the most criticism on is homophobia.

But it's a good example of where we need to be right now. When I speak at homosexual events I tell them two things. First, that when I read the Bible this is what I find and therefore I cannot lend legitimacy to what I believe is contrary to the teaching in the gospel. But second, I want them to know that God loves them anyway and He died for them. I go and preach the gospel.

5

JERRY **WILES**

President, Living Water International

When you come in contact with the people and work of Living Water International, you can leave with only one conclusion—God is at work in a very big problem. Living Water could just tell the story through statistics: There are a billion people on this globe without safe water; at any given time, half of the world's hospital beds are occupied by patients suffering from a water-related disease, resulting in more than 2.2 million deaths per year; more people die each year from drinking dirty water than from the world's hurricanes, floods, tsunamis, and earthquakes combined. But they tell you the story through specific projects in specific places with specific people. This is probably because down deep they care about the people more than they care about the problem.

Christian Buckley: What is your story and the story of Living Water?

Jerry Wiles: We were founded by about five families, including Gary Evans, our executive director, who heads up the field operations, as a result of a

119

mission trip to East Africa in 1990 and 1991. Things really got going in 1994. We've completed more than seven thousand water projects since our founding. I came to Houston in 1991 with the administration of Houston Baptist University. I became acquainted with several of the people who started the organization and came on board in 2003.

CB: As a Christian organization, you seem to be on the cutting edge, engaging with groups like the ONE Campaign, and not just saying we're going to partner with the ONE Campaign, but really taking advantage of what's out there to get your message out. What was the thinking on that?

JW: We don't have to agree with everything to partner with certain kinds of groups. Generally, we kind of feel like there is a common interest—in our case it's clean water. When it comes to the gospel, some people eliminate themselves because they find out we're providing a cup of clean water in Jesus' name. While we do partner a great deal, we try to stay focused on doing what we do with excellence.

CB: Have you found throughout the world that water is a profound evangelical tool, in and of itself?

JW: When you look at the biblical perspective, water is mentioned in the first chapter of Genesis, the last chapter of Revelation, and about five hundred times in between. It is important to God and to people. God created water and He created us such that 70 to 80 percent of our body is made up of water. It is the most basic need of every living creature. In most African, Asian, or Latin American countries, if you were to ask city leaders, government officials, ministers of health, or heads of state, what their five biggest needs are, water will often be at the top. They realize their need for adequate, clean, safe drinking water is a very high priority. When you have a basic understanding of how important water is, you can really connect that with the spiritual reality—the Living Water of Jesus that is life-giving water.

CB: What are your basic goals when you take on a task?

JW: Clean water is the foundation for all sustainable development. If you look at whatever you want to do in the developing world for the kingdom, you can't do health care, economic development, or education very well without clean water. So we're going for the bottom billion—those without clean, safe water. In the course of doing that, we want to integrate the love of Christ in a demonstration along with the appropriate presentation of the gospel wherever we're working. We try to answer the question, "What is the most biblically based, culturally relevant way of bringing the gospel to people and at the same time bringing water?" We don't require people to convert and receive anyone. We don't eliminate or restrict; it's whoever will, may come. There are many examples of going into areas where other religious traditions have not allowed Christians to have access to the water supply. So if we work with a little group of people, get a little piece of property, build a church, drill a water well, and then they freely share their clean, safe drinking water with the Hindus, Muslims, and whoever comes, they begin to ask why we're doing what we're doing. It builds a bridge and opens the door for the gospel in a way that more traditional ways have not been effective.

CB: Let's talk a little more about the practicalities of that if we can. Some would say you could be doing a lot more work if you didn't attach it to the gospel and if you didn't talk about the gospel at all. Others would say that if you only give someone water, but you don't give them the gospel, you have done nothing for them. My guess is that from time to time, you get it from both sides of the aisle. How do you make sure your teams are accomplishing both sides of your goals?

JW: I think first of all, if we were just going to bring water, there's no need for us to exist. There are a lot of organizations that do just water. We just work hard at bringing a balance to it. We're not compelling people to convert. We are coming to help people to get clean, safe drinking water and they know for sure what our motivation is. Our goal is to make sure that every person getting access to clean water through our projects is also getting an appropriate witness. We do that primarily through supporting local churches that will be following up with discipling and continuing the ministry. We also do many other things. We have well dedications where it's proper to do that, where the gospel is always presented by a national, local person. So we're seeking to serve, support, and enable the local churches, and then we work with other mission organizations.

CB: If somebody with a traditional mission mind-set said, "Why not just take the Bible, why take water with the Bible, or why not just take the gospel?" It sounds like your answer might be, "Because it's more effective."

JW: It is more effective, and, to paraphrase an African head of state, "You can't minister to dead people. You can't do health care to dead people. You can't educate dead people. You've got to have them alive first." The first thing is to bring physical life. It is true that if you just bring the water without the message, you just extend their physical life. It's not a matter of either-or with us. It's both-and in every case. It's not a choice. I don't think it's ever the choice of are we going to do just the Word or just the water. I don't think that's ever the option—the gospel or good works. I don't think we have to make that choice because God's going to provide a way to bring the gospel when you engage people and meet their physical needs.

CB: Are there events or images in your mind as you think back over your tenure here that stick out as powerful examples of what you do?

JW: I've got a good number of those. I was just in Liberia for ten days in May. There's been a fourteen-year civil war in Liberia, and about four or five years ago, a little more stability came. In the aftermath there, we have been training ex-combatants in water solutions—drilling, preparing, carpentry, masonry, and literacy programs. Our goal is to begin repairing the infrastructure of this extremely poor country.

There are about three thousand broken hand pumps in the country of Liberia and since we started we have completed with the Liberian nationals one thousand projects—most of which are pump repair and new wells. At the same time, we are doing orality training in the gospel because 80 percent of the population in Liberia is illiterate. We are doing orality workshops and training the local people. More than half of our staff of Liberians are not literate so we are using the storying method to train them to do teamwork and then training them to share these stories and they're going back and sharing these stories in their villages and with their families.

CB: That sounds like a great response to need on more than one level.

JW: One of the things we're trying to avoid is taking a Western culture or an Americanized version of Christianity to the people we're serving and reaching. When we think about 70 percent of the world's population being oral learners—in many of the areas where we're working it's more like 80 to 90 percent—we want to recognize that God is at work in those areas, discover how He is at work, and how we can connect with people in their context, their worldview, and their learning style, and see the gospel take root there.

CB: What would you say is the greatest risk facing Christian humanitarianism as we go forward? Is there a risk that Christianity is being reduced to love and kindness?

JW: I have a concern about this. There are some who would say a demonstration of the love of Christ is adequate. You really don't have to say anything. I don't think you can come up with any biblical basis for that. I think there has to be a show and a tell. I think there always needs to be some form of proclamation and communication of the gospel along with the demonstration of the humanitarian work. I think that can take many forms of expression, but I think if you take the time to study the worldview, understand the culture, look at the bridges, the barriers, and the gaps, you can see how to join God in His activity. Many areas that you go into, you find out that there is already some awareness. God's already brought something there so they don't all need the same thing. I think taking the time to do the research, listen, and build relationships is the key.

CB: As people pick up this project and they read this book and engage, what, above everything else, would you want them to know about Living Water and what you're about?

JW: I would say that God has a place for everybody to be a part of His kingdom and people need to begin engaging in what God's doing through our organization and other organizations.

When it comes down to what we're doing, it is the intervention in people who are dying every day because of water-related diseases. If you can solve the water problem, you can solve a lot of problems. When people can get their heads around how important water is, then you have an opportunity there to talk about the spiritual part of it; it opens the door in a way to engage people that most ministries and missions don't have. Building homes, providing shoes, giving wheelchairs—these are all wonderful things. But when you think about what the most critical physical need on the planet is—it's water.

6

JIM **MORIARTY**

CEO, Surfrider Foundation

Founded in 1984, the Surfrider Foundation is a nonprofit environmental organization dedicated to the protection and enjoyment of our world's oceans, waves, and beaches for all people, through conservation, activism, research, and education. With an annual budget over $5.8 million, Surfrider is one of the largest and most active coastal environmental organizations on the globe. Jim Moriarty, a follower of Christ, sits at the helm of the ship, which gives him an interesting view.

Christian Buckley: I guess the first question I would ask you is, How did your Christian faith inform your decision to take the job at Surfrider?

Jim Moriarty: I was working in high tech, loving that world, when I got a call from a headhunter about the opening. It came out of left field for me. Initially, I didn't really see the fit and told them so, but I loved the mission of Surfrider Foundation and felt there was something compelling me there. The funny thing is that my wife did see the fit and summarized it by saying,

"You were born for that job." As the process continued, I prayed about it and essentially took my hands off the steering wheel. In essence I said, "God, if you want me there . . . put me there." I was an atypical candidate and selection for Surfrider in many ways. By the time they offered me the job, I was convinced God had called me to it.

Now as I look back at the threads in my life, this job really does fit. I've always been drawn to big ideas—big ideas that question the current status quo. The first was probably punk rock. The next one was software, the Web, and the Internet. Environmentalism is in that same vein. Each of these has a world-changing scale. What I did to move from technology into the environment was in some ways a blind step of faith, a step of saying, I am not prepared for this . . . but I'll go anyway. There's a lot of excitement in that. For me, this overlaps with a faith walk, where you are pushed into uncomfortable situations and you come out different on the other side. There's a patina that develops on your soul.

CB: When you joined Surfrider four years ago, was there a certain amount of reticence perhaps on the part of the environmental community toward you? "What are we supposed to make of a Christian who is interested in the environment? Aren't they supposed to be conservative reactionaries who think we're a bunch of hippies?"

JM: Overall, yes. I sometimes feel like I live in a world of non-intersecting circles. In one circle are environmentalists, and in the other circle are Christians.

What I've learned is that the circles can intersect. A person can be both. Regarding the environment, the Christian circle essentially believes that God created the earth, ecosystems, and life itself. The environmentalist circle understands the fragility of our world, importance of intact ecosystems, and the preservation of systems that support life. From my perspective, the circles do overlap, and should overlap more often and with more intellectual and spiritual vigor.

The challenge is that there are people in both circles who can't see the overlapping parts of the circles . . . and instead focus on the differences. If you focus on the non-overlapping parts of the circles, you end up feeling like Christians are indifferent to the state of our environment.

CB: What do you think is at the root of that Christian indifference?

JM: The Christian church has institutional characteristics. There are a lot of factions of the church that put greater emphasis on one area over another. Subjects like environmentalism compete for mind-share with every other possible subject a church can include—disability, military outreach, homelessness, missions, children, and so on. Institutionalizing Jesus' message isn't an easy task because agendas compete and language gets diluted by committees, etc. I think one of the downfalls of the organized church is that certain ideas get relegated or downsized or pushed aside. Environmentalism traditionally has been one of them.

CB: How would you define an *environmentalist*, and would your definition of a Christian environmentalist be any different than your definition of an environmentalist?

JM: Yes, my definitions are different. When I took this job, I told the board, "I'm not an environmentalist" and I specifically said, "I'm not a 'capital E' environmentalist. I am a 'small e' environmentalist," and that's more descriptive of traits that I have and my particular belief system or hierarchy. It's more of a lifestyle and less of a job.

For me, an environmentalist is as simple as someone who understands and appreciates nature and God's creation. I interviewed a seven-year-old girl, Mackenzie Steiner, asking her the silly question, "Are you an environmentalist?" And she said, "I don't know what an environmentalist is." I explained, "Well, it's someone who appreciates God's creation, sees that it's beautiful, and cares for it," to which she quickly said, "I absolutely am that, because fish need clean water and birds deserve clean air." She's right.

A Christian environmentalist is a little bit different because it's more than an appreciation of nature. The Bible offers a context for that appreciation. Many of the people I work with have that appreciation and understanding;

they understand ecosystems, they may understand the science behind them; but they're lacking the context of why they are important. They are important to them because these things sustain life. They are important to me because these things not only sustain life but also they represent the creation over which God gave us stewardship. For me, that adds an extra layer of meaning. For a comparison, think of a non-Christian walking down the street and seeing a beggar and making a decision one way or the other to give the person money. They may say, "I have money and this guy needs some," or they may say, "This guy's a scam artist, I'm not giving him any money." I'd suggest a Christian's perspective would be, "What did Jesus model for us in His words and deeds?" The answer to that question supersedes any reactionary view. The guy might be scamming me, but I'm going to give him money anyway. I'm not going to do it because my buddy's with me. I'm not going to do it because my wife or my kids are with me. I'm going to do it because I follow Jesus. That's the extra layer of context.

CB: How would you respond to those who might argue that Jesus never spoke out about environmental issues? He never fundamentally taught the need to care for creation in the sense that perhaps some in the creation-care movement draw from Genesis and some of the Old Testament obligations.

JM: Building on my last answer . . . I wonder how Jesus would react to the complete annihilation of a species by man, who He charged with taking care of it. The first thing the Bible addresses is creation. It's a pretty amazing story. God created the heavens and the earth and many species of birds, animals, and fish. Why would we destroy that creation?

What I don't understand is why Darwinians are bummed out when a species is lost. That represents survival of the fittest, which is the essence of that theory. Some win. Some lose. Extinction ought to be harder to accept from the Christian perspective. It is an immense sadness to me to think that we wiped anything that God created off the face of the earth. That defies the instructions and mandate He gave to Adam and Eve.

CB: One of the criticisms of environmental and other Christian efforts that don't share the gospel is that they miss the point of hell.

JM: I think that's harsh. Jesus led by example. When I look at Jesus' life, I see Him as a servant. He washed feet and loved people. He put others above Himself, to say the least.

For me, the larger issue is the context for a message. Jesus seemed to really understand this. He was the context for His message. He lived it. We miss this point many times and just try to hammer home a message without the context of love and service, and it comes across as judgmental and harsh. Jesus delivered His message with trust, credibility, and grace.

CB: Right. There's no paradigm. There's no means by which you evaluate those decisions.

JM: A Christian, like it or not, has a very crisp set of boundaries defining right and wrong. You may still sin, but you know that it's wrong. You then seek forgiveness and stop doing it. In addition, we need to get involved in doing God's work and following His calling. I can't do this from behind walls by yelling at people walking by. People need to get out and share their faith. Get dirty. It's messy. The disciples didn't have it easy, and what they risked and sacrificed and did makes typical American church life look pretty darn stagnant by comparison.

CB: So the point of this exercise isn't for Christians to hang out with Christians and wait for the end. The point of the exercise is for God to reach in you and for you to go out there?

JM: Yes. From my perspective that's the larger calling. Some people will say things like, "It's all going to burn anyway; let God sort it out." I find that mind-set to be arrogant. It's as if that individual has the gall to think that they have some intelligence as to when that's going to happen. Whether it's tomorrow or in the twenty-first millennium, they're not going to do anything to preserve what God formed with His own hands. Instead, they're going to destroy it with theirs. Is that what you do with your children? They're going to die anyway. Why invest in them? Why give them food? Why give them good nutrition? Just let them play in the street; let them play in the highways. Give them drugs. They're going to die anyway.

CB: Well, I think that highlights the point you're making about context. It's in God's hands in the absolute eternal sense, but it's also pretty clear that we don't know much about that fact. Why do you think we are so ambivalent about the world around us?

JM: In my opinion, the American culture is out of touch with our surroundings. We're climate controlled. Our children are even more climate controlled. We have beds that go to a certain number. We have offices that go to a certain number. Almost everything is within our control and can be dialed according to our comfort. When you get out in nature, you experience the anti-perfect; everything is shifting. You've got changing microclimates, you've got gale-force winds coming in, you've got huge waves, or you've got complete serenity; but it's changing. Light comes up, light goes down. It's not always on when you press the button. We're not in control; God is. I think we're continuing to insulate ourselves as a culture from the world around us. We have painted ourselves into these tiny little boxes and we don't have the taste for the perspective of creation. We just don't. To really, truly see the utter magnificence of God's creation you need to get outside and do more than go for a walk. What comes to mind for me is snowboarding in absolute whiteouts in Utah or a two-wave hold down in Indonesia. Those kinds of experiences let you know acutely that there are forces much, much more powerful than you at work. The question then becomes, What are these powers? What do I believe about them?

CB: That's interesting. I was having this thought the other morning that we drink so much of the "American" Kool-Aid that we can't separate ourselves from it. Like with my kids, what do I really want from and for my children? Do I really care that they go to college to get a degree, to get a career, to buy a house? Do any of those things make any difference either temporally or eternally? Have I found any satisfaction whatsoever in owning a home or a car? I don't know. Maybe if they were stripped away, I think I'd probably be more satisfied.

JM: You might be.

7

GILBERT **LENNOX**

Pastor and Cofounder, Glenabbey Church of Belfast

Author of *Getting the Message*

When you walk the streets of Belfast or Derry in Northern Ireland you can feel the living history of sectarian violence and division. More than eighty years of unrest have plagued the country where Protestant and Catholic are not merely labels, but identities that for many touch deep-seated emotions of hate, suffering, pain, and loss. *Forgiveness* is not a word frequently found on the lips of those marked by the "troubles," an ironic understatement of the violence that left few untouched in the '60s, '70s, and '80s. Into this cauldron, Gilbert Lennox and several others stepped out in September 1988 to start Glenabbey Church as a response to the New Testament challenge to be a local church—without labels.

Christian Buckley: You were born in Armagh, Northern Ireland. Is that correct?

Gilbert Lennox: Yes.

CB: What was it like growing up there?

GL: Armagh was a much-divided city, still is, but certainly was then. I was a teenager when the first person was shot dead in the so-called troubles. Growing up in Northern Ireland during that time you were shaped in some way by where you lived because how you pronounced various letters of the alphabet in Ireland gave away what your influences were. And the school system was divided. So I went to the state school, which would be regarded by some as a Protestant school, although there were Roman Catholics there.

CB: I would expect—though maybe not—that growing up in Armagh, you must have been personally impacted by the "troubles."

GL: Well, my brother David was blown up in a bomb explosion in '71, and that was traumatic. He almost lost his life. He lost the use of one of his eyes. They were trying to kill British soldiers; they got him instead. Yeah, most families somewhere have been affected in some way by the violence. So yes, that's true.

But it didn't produce in me a hatred of those who had tried to kill my brother. It actually produced a desire to understand what the motivations were. That doesn't mean that I would excuse the offense by any means or that I don't hate the actual thing that they did; but I tried to understand what motivated people to do that on both sides of it, and again, my sense was that the only solution or answer to the issues was found in Christ.

CB: Did the events in your brother's life impact your understanding of God's call in your life, the presence or potential, you might say, that at any time something might happen?

GL: Oh, I'm sure it impacts everyone. I had the privilege of my upbringing; financially, my father was a businessman, so I had quite a sheltered upbringing. It was easier for me to process the "troubles" at the theoretic level as opposed to living on a street that was regularly being raided by the British Army, with the floorboards being ripped up. However justified the searches may have been, there was still a lot of abuse, fear, and so on. I never personally experienced that. When I went to university in the early seventies in Belfast, most of my friends came from very different contexts. They were coming from, most of them, areas in Belfast that were clearly identified with one side of the sectarian divide or the other. And talking with them and learning to understand what it was like to be on the receiving end of searches by the army and so on helped me to see the other side to the issues.

CB: And then, in 1988, you started this church with a band of others in New Town Abbey, and that, according to my wife, is north of Belfast?

GL: Yes, yes. It is.

CB: So why? What was the catalyst within you to start a nondenominational religious institution in an area where that concept must still be, and certainly in 1988 must have been, almost nonsensical to most people?

GL: Probably the early catalyst for me would have been my parents, my upbringing. My parents were not sectarian. My father was a businessman and sought to employ more or less equal numbers of Protestants and Catholics in Armagh. It was a very brave and courageous stand to take based on his religious convictions; he was nonpolitical and nonsectarian. That was quite formative for my thinking during my teenage and university years. I developed an interest in the local church as something other than what I had experienced of sectarianism in the areas where I grew up, of the denominational labels that are still there.

But the actual catalyst to the formation of this new church was a deep conviction that we wanted something where people could unite in Christ from all sides of the community. That the unifying thing was the gospel, was Christ, that didn't have a denominational label.

CB: I assume there were some obvious roadblocks to the idea.

GL: Sure. In our context, especially for folks coming from a Roman Catholic background, to go to a Presbyterian church, to a Baptist church, to a Brethren church . . . was to associate with a different culture. It's not just a matter of coming to faith in Christ and worshiping Him in our church with others. Leaving a church, Protestant or Catholic, is almost betraying your own culture. It would indeed be seen that way by many.

Even the very fact of setting up an independent church was seen then by Protestant denominations, even though it's changed a little now, as a very doubtful operation, as some kind of a cult. And then from a Catholic perspective, it would have been seen as some Protestant weird thing because one of the things they struggle with when they look at Protestantism is the number of different labels of denominations.

CB: How did you deal with that?

GL: We sought to establish something where folks could come without the label over the door and be accepted as human beings, created in the image of God, in Christ.

CB: Was that why your church was planted in a warehouse? I suppose there's a practical side to that and perhaps a wise side, that it bears no institutional markings. What went into that thought process?

GL: The warehouse was not particularly artistic or inspiring from the point of view of a "church," but nobody would know it was a church building, and for us that was important. It is very much what you said from a number of points of view, not just because of the sectarian divisions in the country and denominationalism, but also our real aim was to seek to reach people who have either been hurt by the church or turned off Christ in some way because of what they saw in the church—people for whom church was not answering the questions that they were asking.

CB: Have you seen the notion of having a direct relationship with God, with Christ, as something that is productive for people in working through the conflicts rather, than saying your relationship to God is through a church, and then that church becomes ideologically linked to years of suffering and violence and hatred and everything else that's imbued with the "troubles"? Have you seen that work? Do you have a belief that it can be an effective bridge?

GL: Yes. That's the heart of the gospel. It's reconciling. In our context, my own feeling is that can be done more easily when you try to strip away some of the cultural barriers that have existed for so long. But you can't do that completely and I wouldn't claim that. But fundamentally, yes, people meet in Christ. That's a great way of stripping the barriers—understanding the nature of the body of Christ, which is not denominationally determined, but spiritually determined. That's huge for folks to understand—the church is fundamentally that.

CB: Do you think the church, however we would define that, has a duty to be active in the work of political or racial reconciliation? Is there an independent duty? And maybe secondarily, have you felt pressure—as obviously your church has grown—have you felt pressure to more formally become involved in that process?

GL: Yes, there has been some pressure in that. Quite a number of churches have been involved in various initiatives like that. My own instinct and perhaps my own theology—at least I hope it's coming from theology and not just personal bias—is to be wary of the formal attempt to do that. I don't discourage folks from being involved and following their convictions there, but I tend to think that people lose their way very often in the political/social activity because the gospel can get lost and then the work becomes purely social activity. I think it's important to be good citizens, but when it comes to the gospel, once you tie the gospel or even seem to tie the gospel to a particular political approach, I think you then ultimately weaken the gospel.

I came to know a person from the Republican side of the divide, who had been in prison at the time of the famous Hunger Strike and who had since come to faith in Christ.[2] His approach was one of "little ripples"—impacting one life at a time, working at the micro level of society.

He invited me to speak at a retreat in a monastery, actually quite near my hometown, so I thought, This is wonderful irony—speaking in a Catholic monastery. I had an absolutely phenomenal time with him and his friends. I think there were almost thirty of us in all. They came from the strongly Republican and Catholic areas of Belfast and had discovered Jesus, found forgiveness and new life in Him, and were seeking to follow Him as Catholic believers. It was marvelous to be with them and see their approach, just working one life at a time, caring for people, loving people. They had no big program of social action in the formal sense, but they did a lot at the individual and family level to influence their neighbors. Pretty much the way I think Jesus told us to do it.

CB: So you would be less in favor of taking a social approach to your work.

GL: Our church is positively involved in community initiatives both in Northern Ireland and overseas, but I am generally cautious in those things. I've enough awareness of church history to know that what often starts out extremely well can end up where the gospel itself gets lost—people lose the motivation. The humanitarian side is what's left and, you know, that's ultimately not what survives. I think with the early church the Jewish authorities would have been very happy if the Christians had confined themselves to so-called good works. But they were very upset when they insisted in doing them in the name of Jesus. That's where the problem was. I think that the problem is still there.

A couple of years ago, I was talking to a group that was very much involved in reconciliation-type activity, and they talked to me a lot about doing the works of Christ and demonstrating the kingdom. So I listened and watched and a lot of the work they were doing was excellent in itself and valid and valuable and I wouldn't decry it, but I asked them, "Do you ever get around to sharing the words of Christ?" and they said, "No."

CB: Many have said that the church in Europe is dwindling. Is that true in your area, and if so, why?

GL: I think the presence of the peace process, increasing secularism, increasing materialism, has seen people just disappear. The opportunities for entertainment in the city, especially Belfast, has transformed it, and much of that I welcome, but it's just a European, secular city that gives young people so much more choice. They look at their faith, their parents' and their grandparents', and it's just completely irrelevant to their life.

CB: That's interesting. Are you saying that with respect to the peace, at least the 2007 peace, that the presence of peace is reducing the importance of church?

GL: Yes. I would say so, but I don't know how you would test that. It's just the sense I have that the increase in wealth leads to a drift away from the church. This has happened in the rest of the UK and the same trends may be happening here.

CB: So is this the generation that will turn things around once and for all?

GL: I think there is a new generation of younger people who are taking Scripture seriously; they are taking the gospel seriously. They haven't got into the more materialistic, self-centered values of previous generations. And that is really thrilling to see. I hope that will turn things around. I think the denominationalism will become harder to sustain, especially if the church is really faithful to Christ and loyal—the lines will be more clearly drawn and a lot of folks will see the denominationalism disappear.

CB: Well, I appreciate that you're doing the Lord's work on the ground, in the trenches, in a very difficult place in the world to do it—culturally, politically, sociologically . . .

GL: But I'm no sociologist, as I'm sure you see. I get up and do my best to teach the Bible every weekend and speak into folks' lives, and that's what I profoundly believe in.

8

FRANKLIN GRAHAM

President and CEO, Samaritan's Purse

Author of *Rebel With a Cause* and *The Name; Living Beyond the Limits*

It would be hard to overstate the shadow cast by Franklin Graham's father, especially where preaching the gospel is concerned. But Franklin appears to be right at home in his own preaching of the gospel, both in word and deed, as he heads one of the largest gospel-centered humanitarian organizations on the globe (over $300 million in support and revenues in 2008).

Christian Buckley: What is the difference between humanitarian work and Christian humanitarian work?

Franklin Graham: In the Sermon on the Mount Jesus said, "Blessed are the merciful." All believers should pray to be vessels of mercy toward others—first to the household of faith—our brothers and sisters in Christ around the world, and then to those who do not know Him as their Savior. Christians who do good deeds without the foundation of Scripture are operating in the name of humanitarianism. The Word of God is the backbone of Christian service. Jesus said that His followers are the salt of the earth and

143

He is the Bread of Life. It is important for Christians to continually renew their commitment to the commands of Christ—to live obedient lives and use the abilities He gives us to serve others with compassionate spirits. Christ enables us to do this through the power of His Holy Spirit that works in us and through us.

It never hurts to rehearse the Great Commission, "to go into the whole world and preach the gospel." While Christ fed the multitudes and healed individual wounds and sickness, He did so for the purpose of making Himself known to those who were seeking peace from their suffering, from their hunger and thirst, and from their total despair. Christ did not call us to feed people. Christ did not call us to heal people. His followers are called to take His gospel to the hungry, sick, lonely, tormented, and lost. The object of our service toward others is Christ, for He is the only One who can quench thirst, alleviate hunger, and touch the soul with the salve of forgiveness, comfort, and love. That "salve" is the very blood He shed upon the cross for the sins of the world. Through His lifesaving blood we are able to receive all He offers us through His sacrifice.

We must remember that there are many organizations that receive funding and do good works. But when they feed empty bellies, they'll have to keep feeding them lest they starve. No organization can continue to feed the same millions year after year. But when people's souls are fed, when they are nourished by the Word of God, God will bless those who are dispensing His goodness, and He will bless the needy when they put their trust in Him. He will meet their greatest need and give them abundant life in Him.

CB: What do you think is the state of Christian humanitarian investment now as opposed to five or ten years ago?

FG: While many churches across our country have increased their humanitarian outreach in the name of their communities, their mission programs are shrinking. I believe that the focus on providing human needs has diminished the message we are supposed to carry as good Samaritans. The parable that Jesus told about the Good Samaritan is certainly at the core of the work we do at Samaritan's Purse. Our purpose in responding to crises around the world is not to help the government provide housing and soup kitchens for refugees, our purpose is to work with people through the storms that beset them to earn the right to proclaim the love of Jesus Christ. This is what compels us to meet the needs of others and to do it unashamedly.

Paul said in Romans 1:16 that he was not ashamed of the gospel because it is the power of God unto salvation. Why would he declare he was not ashamed unless there were people of that day who *were* ashamed of God's message? Ashamed to admit their sin? Ashamed to tell others that sin separates all men from God? Ashamed to admit that Christ is the only answer for every problem man encounters on earth?

Humanitarianism will not save one soul from hell. Only through the gospel—God's message to all—can man be saved. God empowers His Word to forgive sinners and transform their minds, hearts, and souls. I believe the church needs to carefully and thoughtfully declare the motive of its good works toward others. Our motive should be single-minded: to reach out in the name of the Lord Jesus Christ and pray that others will see Christ who lives in us.

CB: Those are powerful words. It seems quite personal for you.

FG: My grandfather, Dr. L. Nelson Bell, was a missionary doctor in China for twenty-five years. In the early twentieth century a door of opportunity was opened for him and my grandmother to serve the Chinese people in this vast, un-evangelized country. As a leader in the Presbyterian denomination, the church supported his monumental decision to serve the Lord in China. While my grandfather was obedient to investing his life in the Chinese people, the church made enormous investments in China and built a large mission hospital operated by my grandfather. But my grandfather did not transplant himself from America to China for the purpose of bringing medicine to the sick, but rather he uprooted his family for the purpose of bringing the light of the gospel into a spiritually depraved society. He performed surgery and treated human frailties so that God's message might penetrate the darkened hearts of the lost. When my grandparents were forced out of the country decades later, they could never be certain how many souls had been won for Christ, but in my visits to China long after they were in heaven I have met multitudes of people who came to Christ because of his ministry through medicine, and the Christian population in China today is greater than it's ever been, though they continue under suppression and forms of persecution.

Samaritan's Purse is doing much the same today in Sudan. We have a team of doctors, nurses, teachers, pastors, and Bible teachers working throughout Sudan with a specific focus on Darfur, a place that has finally gained some outcry from the world due to the tremendous suffering of predominantly black Christians living in a Muslim stronghold. Our team members understand our purpose for being there and God has blessed as His Word is faithfully being proclaimed as they go about their day-to-day duties in His great and mighty name.

This is the key: Everything must be done in the name of the Lord Jesus. When we begin to brush God to the side because it might offend someone, our purpose is gone. The people who support the work of Samaritan's Purse don't send contributions just to feed the hungry. They want assurance that their hard-earned money is going to sow the gospel seed into barren hearts and empty souls. This door opens through feeding programs and medical clinics.

Some people ask, "Franklin, aren't you taking advantage of people who are hurting?" I respond, "Did the Good Samaritan take advantage of the poor soul he pulled out of the dirt alongside the road?" No. He took personal responsibility to see that this man received the best of care until he could get back on his feet. He sacrificed his time and money because his motive was selfless.

Making the most of an opportunity is quite different from taking advantage of those less fortunate. But I will say, there is a lot of red tape involved when someone reaches out to help another. But we persevere because we are compelled by the love of Christ. Jesus didn't come to give us a better world. He didn't come to save us from leprosy or cancer. He came to save our lost souls by the sacrifice of Himself—the shedding of His blood to cover our sins and restore our fellowship to His Father, our Creator and Lord. The gospel power is plugged into the Source who sits on the heavenly throne observing His children in action. That action is effective for Christ when the deeds are done for Him, by Him, and He accomplishes all of this through His own—followers in His Son, Jesus Christ.

CB: What was the catalyst in your heart for writing a recent letter entitled "Now Is the Time for Evangelism"?

FG: Our country is changing. There should be an urgency to preach the gospel. Five years from now we may not have the freedom to preach in the name of Christ. In some countries like Australia, some preachers went to prison a few years ago because they spoke out against Islam. Here in America, the day is coming when Christians may be imprisoned for speaking out against homosexuality, for instance. We are commanded by the Lord to speak the truth in love. But the world doesn't want to hear the truth. They believe they have the truth—their truth is what they make it. Our truth is foundational—in the Lord Jesus Christ. He is the "way, the truth, and the life." Why shouldn't Christians who carry the greatest and most freeing message ever want to spread it as far and wide as possible? Christians around the world have become martyrs for holding to their faith regardless of the consequences. Christians in America have known little of this kind of sacrifice, but rapidly we are losing the freedoms we've taken for granted. The media has had some victories in painting Christians as intolerant—not the left radicals. The day is coming when the enemies of the cross will do whatever it takes to silence the gospel.

The Scripture says, "Now is the day of salvation." This has been a long day—from the day of the cross until the present. But the urgency is found in this word "now." The Bible says, "Exhort one another daily, while it is called 'today'" (Hebrews 3:13).

CB: How do you keep your compass aligned on evangelism as your primary task?

FG: We never take on a project at Samaritan's Purse unless we are able to present it in the name of the Lord Jesus Christ. That makes the decision process almost seamless. If we can't preach the Word of God, there are many organizations that can step in to meet human need. My goal is to step into tragedies where God's Word can be presented and heard. This is our compelling task. Samaritan's Purse was founded by the late Dr. Bob Pierce.[3] This was his burning desire: to preach Christ to the suffering. This was his DNA. This is my DNA.

It does concern me when I see young people today zealous to do "good deeds." It is commendable that their hearts are pliable, but I worry that their mentors, perhaps even many church leaders, are not laying the spiritual grounding that is needed for their deeds to be used of God to accomplish His purpose—not to save physical life, but to redeem repentant souls for His kingdom. Multitudes of young people today are not getting this vitally important truth. I hear youth today talk about raising money to go and help people in Africa for a week, or to go and rock AIDS babies for a few days, but there is no purpose in their "work" other than to experience international travel or have a story to tell. Or more frightening, they think this is what makes them a Christian and gives them the right to heaven after life on earth. People may have good intentions to travel abroad to help the dying or reach out to their neighbor at home, but if the help is not motivated by the gospel message, their works will burn in the fire of eternity. If we don't proclaim Christ to the lost, what have we really accomplished?

CB: As you look back at your tenure at Samaritan's Purse, is there anything that haunts you when you put your head on your pillow at night?

FG: To be honest, I prefer to look ahead. Paul said in Scripture, "Press toward the mark." I lean in the forward direction because there's little that can be changed about the past. However, there is value in looking back and learning from mistakes, or simply learning how to do something better or more effectively, based on experience. Certainly the New Testament spends a great deal of time "looking back" to the Old Testament. The Old Testament prophesied about things to come and the New Testament was the fulfillment of the great prophecies. We would have little to rejoice about if we couldn't *look back*. So, I never want to stop learning, but while my mind may be contemplating the past and what can be learned from it, I hope my steps will never stop moving forward.

I remember the early days of Operation Christmas Child. The idea of packing shoeboxes for children living in war zones in Bosnia was developed by a man in England. He called me one day years ago and asked if I would donate some shoeboxes for his cause. I told him I would. As December approached, he called to see how many I had collected. I had forgotten all about it. I bought a little more time and called a pastor friend in Charlotte, North Carolina, and told him about my predicament and asked for help. He rallied his church and within a couple of weeks he had collected eleven thousand shoeboxes. I was stunned. We were able to ship them in time for Christmas. But when I followed up on the project later, I learned that the boxes had been distributed, but there was no evangelism component built into the program at all. In time, the entire project was put into our care and the first thing we did was to design the collection and distribution of the shoebox gifts around the gospel, utilizing the truth of the Christ child as the greatest gift ever given. It was this component that turned a simple shoebox gift program into the largest children's Christmas project in the world. We have learned from past mistakes and every year the program has swelled to now encompass a follow-up discipleship program with over three million kids involved in a Bible correspondence school.

CB: How do you respond to those who say, "We don't preach the gospel because it would limit the number of partners we could take on and the amount of funding we could get."

FG: That mind-set tells me that Christ is not at the center of their outreach. They are doing work in the name of humanitarianism. These groups likely seek funding from the government. While Samaritan's Purse has been the recipient of some government funding for large programs, we are not willing to change the core of our work. While we cannot spend government dollars on evangelism, it doesn't mean that we can't use government funds for food and clothing, and then raise additional funds for Christian literature and other tools that help us present Christ to the lost.

We live in a world of compromise. And I'm afraid to say that many churches today are compromising their spending, their programming, and even their preaching in order to attract the world's attention. They want to be loved and adored by the world. They seek the world's approval. The Bible says, "Do not love the world or the things in the world" (1 John 2:15). God warns in the book of Revelation that these things will be judged.

CB: Do you see any difference between the work you're doing and the legacy of your father?

FG: I have said many times that I cannot fill the shoes of Billy Graham. No one can, nor does God expect us to fill another's shoes. God deals with each of His children uniquely. He has a specific work for every individual. When you read the great biographies in Scripture, not one of God's servants lived the same experience. Every story is uniquely different. This is one of the many components that make Bible reading thrilling and adventuresome. God knows us by name and has a different job for everyone who serves Him. While I have assumed the leadership of my father's evangelistic organization in addition to continuing with the work of Samaritan's Purse, I want to be obedient to my calling as a preacher of the gospel and use every opportunity to proclaim His message to a dying world, whether it is in a stadium in North America or in African villages. I've been blessed to couple these components together and watch God work in miraculous ways.

CB: Given the reach of Samaritan's Purse and your experience of doing humanitarian or relief work, what is the difference between doing that work and doing that work well?

FG: Many organizations—and individuals—travel abroad these days. Many are sincere in their desire to help those in need, but when they get there the needs are overwhelming and they simply don't know where to start. Their hearts may be in the right place, but they don't have a clue where to begin. Others go for the thrill of it, only to return home and forget what touched them, perhaps, for the time they were there—to see the despair of refugees, war victims, or orphans roaming the streets. Too many send missionary teams out for a week or two, make a lot of promises in the name of the Lord, come home and raise money and often it never gets to the foreign field but rather is redirected to meet a social need in the home church or organization. This may not be their original intent, but it happens, and it is a reproach on the name of the Lord Jesus.

Our approach has been to go, assess, commit, return home, and let God's people know what we observed and how God touches the heart to help. If God is in it, we will trust Him for the funds to carry out the work. Jesus Himself said, "For which of you, intending to build a tower, does not sit down first and count the cost, whether he has enough to finish it, lest, after he has laid the foundation, and is not able to finish, all who see it begin to mock him" (Luke 14:28–29). We are accountable to the Lord, and He holds us accountable. When we come up short, we give bad witness to the One we serve. We represent the King of Kings. For this reason alone, we should hold the standard high and do everything in a way that will bring glory and honor to Him. This is the work that He can and will bless—when the goal is to lift His name up high so that all can see "by His hand it has been accomplished" (1 Kings 8:15).

CB: Lastly, where do you see the greatest need in the world right now?

FG: That question has several answers. From a spiritual perspective, I believe the greatest weakness is within the church in America. It has all the trappings that Christ warns about in His letters to the seven churches found in the Revelation. Apostasy is permeating our churches. There is a great need to return to the true doctrine in Scripture.

My father talks often about the late Dr. Alan Redpath who served as pastor of the great Moody Church in Chicago. On his desk was a plaque that said "Beware of the Barrenness of a Busy Life." The church has been so busy with trying new methods and programs that they have failed in studying Scripture and the doctrines that Christ set forth as the central message of church ministry. As a result, it has given entrance to false teaching that has seeped into the pulpits—pews being filled by empty souls thinking they have a reservation in heaven because of their "busy" works. People are being misled by false teachers just as the Bible predicted would happen in the last days.

Another answer to your question could be directed, again, toward the misunderstanding of humanitarian work related to human suffering. No one person, no one organization can alleviate all of these problems. This will not be accomplished until Christ returns. But we must do what we can. I believe that the Lord places our footsteps in the paths that He has designed for us. We are responsible to be alert and be looking for His signs that move us down those paths in obedience, swinging open the doors that at first seem to be closed. As we move step-by-step, He guides us by His Holy Spirit. That's why so much of our work is unpredictable. The Holy Spirit goes ahead of us and many times He has to wait for us to catch up because we're not paying attention, we're not seeking Him, we're not watching the path where He has placed our footsteps.

For me, this was certainly the case when it came to committing Samaritan's Purse to the work we are doing in Sudan. I had no idea, at first, what Samaritan's Purse could possibly do in the midst of such carnage. When I began to cross paths with people from Sudan and others who were hearing about the persecution taking place, my heart was drawn to the overwhelming needs—not to mention the opportunity for the gospel. Black Muslims in Sudan were mercilessly murdering black Christians. They were destroying churches across the land, ethnic cleansing was intended to purge the country of all Christians, and they were having great success.

I often think about the Macedonian call the apostle Paul received, saying, "Come and help us." I felt like this with Sudan and God wonderfully opened up one door at a time and has allowed Samaritan's Purse to make an impact in His name with the gospel of freedom found in Jesus Christ. This is what makes doing relief work worthwhile. Without this fundamental purpose and goal—to reach the lost for Christ—relief work would be impossible, because it can never be solved. When one crisis is over, another arises, and it will be this way until the end of time. So this is why I say, "Now is the time for evangelism." *Now* is the operative word when it comes to evangelism.

9

GARY **HAUGEN**

President and CEO, International Justice Mission
Author of *Just Courage; Good News About Injustice*

There exists an intensity in the eyes of every great lawyer who knows what it takes to win. It is that extra force of nature that quietly tells the opposition, "You can beat me or fight me, but you won't outlast me." It was the first thing I noticed in Gary Haugen when we sat down in his D.C. office. Gary started International Justice Mission (IJM) in 1997 after returning from his United Nations appointment to head the investigation of the Rwandan Genocide.[4] There is no question that he brought the credentials and experience to do the job, but he brought something else with him that palpably filled the offices and staff of IJM on the day I was there.

Christian Buckley: When you wake up every day, what are you waking up to do? What is, "This is what I'm about"?

Gray Haugen: I think every day is about living a life in God. That is to say, my life has been given to me by God and has been given to me for a purpose and a way of living that is His. And so every day is about living in that life that He has given and invited me to. And that is pretty much summed up by Jesus by living a life of love for God and a life of love for others. As far as I can tell that's pretty much it.

CB: Did you grow up wanting to do what you do now or was there a point when the light switched on for you?

GH: No, it was a very incremental process. It is a paradox that so much of my life now with International Justice Mission in recent years has been dwelling in these places of great suffering and violence, brutality, and evil in the world because I grew up in a place that couldn't have been further from all of that. I grew up in a nice suburb of Sacramento, California, in a nice Christian home, going to church and all the rest. But I did have an earnest yearning for God and by the time I was in college there seemed to be something I didn't understand of intimacy with God. My world was very, very limited, very, very sheltered from the massive reality of human suffering in the world. I had this sense that I really wanted to know God more deeply, but there are whole parts of who He is and who I am that I was just not even getting to because I was living outside this deep reality of the world.

So it started as this very incremental toe-in-the-water process of taking steps to experience human suffering and hurt in the world. Once you're there, you have to start asking the questions: What does it mean to be alive to God? To love Him and love my neighbor here? That just got incrementally challenging, and incrementally interesting, and incrementally powerful. God made Himself so manifest in those places that the thirst was fed by that and continued to proceed incrementally in that way.

CB: So in '97 you left the United States Justice Department and found yourself here. Was there anything fundamentally different in what you did then and what you do now? Obviously you were in Rwanda as a state/UN official. Now you are fighting the same or maybe different injustices, but you're doing it from a different chair. What's fundamentally different?

GH: The thing that is different is that I am doing it in a community of fellow believers. I'm doing it in an intentional Christian community of prayer and spiritual formation.

The other thing that is different is I have a sense of missional purpose in inviting the rest of the body of Christ likewise into the work. This was not what I did previously. The technical work is in many ways very, very similar, but I'm choosing to do it in Christian community, largely for my own sense of health and well-being and sustenance in doing it. I have done this work in the absence of Christian prayerful community and one's a lot better than the other for me. The other is this sense of missional purpose in wanting to invite and encourage the rest of the body of Christ to do these things as well.

CB: It strikes me, as someone who grew up in big churches, fairly read in theology, fairly aware of global issues, that the awareness and understanding of the issues of slavery, injustice, and sexual trafficking is a tenth of what it should be, given the severity of the problems. I don't know the exact statistics, but people say there are twenty-seven million slaves in the world. Some say thirty. There are about thirty million people in the world who are afflicted with AIDS. Here we have two numbers that are not hugely disproportionate to each other, and yet there's an immense disproportion in what the Christian community understands, wakes up knowing, wakes up thinking about. Why? What don't we get?

GH: I think there are a lot of different answers to that. One of them is that we have a really hard time looking at problems we don't know how to do anything about. It's hard to give a lot of attention and focus to some brutal, ugly problems, after which everybody says, "Isn't that horrible? Darn. Too bad." That's completely disempowering.

It's very easy for us to be focused in our own little world. Our little world is stressful enough. We're just trying to get our kids to school. We're trying to not mess up our own lives. It's stressful. So the idea of seeing things out beyond our border is just naturally not easy. But then let's say I do get your attention to look at this; what I don't do is tell you what you could possibly do about it. In other categories of human suffering and need, Christians have been equipped with substantial visions of what they can actually *do*. You can sponsor a child. You can provide microfinance. You can establish a clinic. But in the area of violence and the brutal oppression of another human being that's intentional and has real bad guys behind it, no one ever explained what you can actually do and what actually can work. IJM has begun to introduce it a little bit differently, to say, "Oh, no, no, no, let's deconstruct the problem for you a little bit; it looks scary and overwhelming, but actually you can do something about it"—and look, God actually shows up and does something about it. Now it's okay to look at how terrible it is because we don't have to be left in that despair. We can do something about it.

CB: One of the questions I get all the time in doing death penalty work is, "What's that like?" I rarely try to answer that question for people, but one of the things that's dawned on me is that there is an insight of the human condition. It looks me straight in the eye and says, "This is the ravages of sin." It's the lowest common denominator. That's something you also face. To know not just that people are being made sex slaves and traded, but that there's an entire group of people out there who are doing the trading. You face two constituencies—the oppressed and the oppressor. When you look at the oppressor, what does it tell you about the human condition? How has that impacted your view of the world?

GH: It certainly makes the sometimes rather dry, abstract teaching of the Bible on the fallen nature of the world become very, very vivid. We're not problem solving the fallen nature of the world, not managing it. The reality that human beings can turn their back on God and He has allowed room for the very aggressive temptations of evil is not working well. It is working out so badly, you can't even imagine it unless you go and see it. That's why the Rwandan genocide is one of those experiences that everyone should study—the Holocaust or the Cambodian genocide—because it's very normal human beings who are capable of stepping over a line, where yesterday they were a normal neighbor and today they are a mass murderer of perfectly innocent people. It's not a hard line for normal human beings to cross. Human beings can wake up every day and intentionally and precisely organize their day so that girls can be serially raped or people can be beaten and abused. The human capacity for this should not be misunderstood and all of our attempts to imagine that human beings are basically managing without their Maker are not true. Whether that's the quiet, little nasty pettiness, selfishness, and brutality inside in suburban homes or mass genocide, it's the same utter brokenness where human beings really do need a Savior.

CB: In what way is the issue of slavery or justice a uniquely Christian issue? Is it different for a Christian because they're drawing on a different well?

GH: It's harder for me to generalize for all Christians or for all people, but for me personally, I think the capacity to do the work of justice requires the capacity to love. Not as love cheaply bought or sentimentalized, but to do for them what you would want done for you, irrespective of the costs. And people who are suffering under injustice, if you're going to love them, you're going to have to risk a substantial amount because there is a cost for doing it. I think it's very hard to actually love victims of brutal injustice because you're going to have to insert yourself between the victim and the strongman, and for me the only capacity to do that comes from intimacy with God, drawing upon His power to love like that. For me to be able to love the way the victim of injustice needs me to love them, I'm going have to stay very close to the source of love. That's what my brothers and sisters at IJM and I find in community together—an intimacy with the God of love and God of justice that allows us to walk that way.

CB: How do you love the oppressor? It's not often talked about. We get the need to love the oppressed, that girl that's been traded and traded and used up, but don't tell me that I need to love the person who enslaved, and yet Christ exemplified that kind of love. That's pretty revolutionary. The secular wisdom is, that's the evil person and that's the good person. Christian wisdom says, fundamentally, we're all evil people. We all need to be loved—found. How has that worked out in your own life?

GH: The first thing is to restrain them from oppressing others. It's not good for their soul to commit violence and abuse and egregious sin against a neighbor. We have to restrain that impulse. It isn't loving to continue to allow the husband who is beating his wife to keep beating his wife. It's not good for the husband or his wife. It's actually good to hold his arm and stop him from doing it. It also provides a powerful opportunity for repentance, for turning another way. That's part of what you do see when you bring justice or accountability to bear on perpetrators. It's not always the case, but there is this confrontation with the reality for that perpetrator from which they were allowed to excuse themselves for a period of time. There is right and wrong. There are consequences in the universe for them. In the absence of accountability, they're allowed to be kept by their spiritual enemy in a fantasy world. Mostly what I see when we bring perpetrators to account and they're handcuffed and walking off to jail—a nasty place for them, for a long time—you can almost always see the brokenness, despair, utter weakness. While they might have been feeling very powerful and proud while they were raping and abusing some thirteen-year-old girl, they don't feel any of that in those moments. It is a flash of reality for them that is better for their soul than the horror for themselves they were actually in before.

I also know that those perpetrators were all born as babies, somebody hopefully loved them and wanted them to have a life that was alive to God, and they were intended for that. It is much more a triumph of the Enemy and the evil in the world that their lives have become so twisted that they do what they do. But they were not created for that. There isn't any perpetrator that I look at that I say, "That's what you were created for."

CB: Switching gears, to play the devil's advocate, one question frequently asked is where the gospel is in what you're doing. How do you respond?

GH: It's encouraging that I hear that question less and less. That's a really good sign. In many ways, it's like the question, "If you're exhaling, when are you going to inhale, and if you're inhaling, when are you going to exhale?" Well, you're supposed to do both things—it's called breathing. Likewise, where's the gospel? The gospel is good news—so gospel is in the proclamation of affirmative truth, but it is also in the demonstration of what one is speaking of. The good news is that God loves you. Well, for the twelve-year-old girl who's getting raped in a brothel, for me to come and say to her, "God loves you," just doesn't seem to have much meaning or credibility because God doesn't seem very loving. She would probably reply, "Are you kidding? How could He possibly love me? He's letting this happen to me. And how could *you* possibly be loving me, because you're letting it happen?" It doesn't mean very much at all.

On the other hand, if we were to pretend that it's sufficient in our love for others to simply meet physical needs without endeavoring to introduce or invite them to their Maker, the One who made them and loves them, then that's utterly incomplete. I don't want to just exhale, I don't want to just inhale—I actually want to *breathe*, and that's what I think it means to love our neighbor.

CB: What has been your experience with the politicizing of "Christianity" in America? We seem to define "Christianity" based on what we need it to be. Are you seeing a change in this definition now versus, say, five years ago?

GH: I do think there is a cost that is paid when mere Christianity is hitched to or forced to align itself with a matter of public policy that really is not at the core or part of mere Christianity. In one respect, it's important for the followers of Jesus to be engaged in the political process. It's part of our stewardship of power that we have as voting citizens in the United States. Whenever God gives us power, it's meant to be stewarded for His purposes. It's meant to be engaged. But if one is using the moral power of their Christian identification and then trying to push a matter of particular policy agenda, there are risks associated with that. That's what I think is a challenge. To the extent that the Christian gospel has been associated with one political point of view or the other, it then does create an obstacle to those who don't share that policy point of view, but might really share the mere Christianity on the inside.

CB: Finally, there seem to be a growing number of organizations—Christian or otherwise—that are beginning to engage in human trafficking issues.

What in your experience is the difference between doing the work and doing it well?

GH: I see the difference in three key areas. First, it's accountability to outcomes. What are you trying to do? Are you really achieving that outcome? The temptations are to be unclear about what you're trying to do so that if you shoot enough you hit it every time, or to move the goal because it starts to get hard. "Let's not really rescue them out of the brothel, but let's have a conference to let everyone know who they are in the brothel because actually getting them out is too hard." It's moving the goalpost. There's no actual accountability to the people at the end of the line.

These humanitarian matters are about loving your neighbor. So let's go find a neighbor and find out whether that neighbor actually would say they were really well loved—that it mattered to them, there was an outcome that mattered to them. You have to have actual accountability to the neighbor for effectively loving them.

A second huge part of the IJM mission is transparency. We can all agree that transparency is a good thing—but it's hard. Even the church community many times may not be open and transparent, but it's an integral part of doing good work well and it's something we can all work on.

Humility is the third thing. We have to have an authentic humility that is learning all the time, stepping up to own our mistakes, and trying to get better.

I think where you have accountability to outcomes, transparency, and humility matched with a zeal for excellence—people are loved well.

10

RUSTY **PRITCHARD**

Founder and President, Flourish

Rusty Pritchard, founder and president of Flourish, is passionate about the environment and the impact it has on our lives. His organization exists to inspire and equip churches "to better love God by reviving human lives and the landscapes on which they depend"—a decidedly a-political mission and message. With a background in environmental academics, research, policy, ministry, and consulting, he is well qualified to address creation care from a Christian perspective, and it would seem that he continues to find the overwhelming truth that God, through His creation, is still transforming hearts and minds one person at a time.

Christian Buckley: Why is environmentalism considered a political issue and yet that's less the case with homelessness, poverty, hunger, or disease?

Rusty Pritchard: It didn't really start out that way. The Clean Water Act, the Clean Air Act, the creation of the EPA—those things happened with bi-partisan support under several presidents. It hasn't been a historical divide, and for a lot of people it has never become a liberal-conservative divide. For example, the Hunter-Angler movement has been portrayed as right wing, but many of those people are very concerned about the places where they grew up and the heritage of outdoor sports. They vote for land conservation and actively work and invest in protecting them. They are actually out in those places, concerned with those places, exposed to those places. So it's still not as left/right as you might think when you get down to the local level.

But on the national level, I think the left likes to beat the right up on environmental stuff as a useful political weapon, and so they never talk about all of the great progress we've made environmentally and the environmental protections that we've enjoyed in cleaning up the environment. They prefer to paint a picture of crisis and intransigence from the right. People on the right like to beat up people on the left as anti free-market, and they don't like to talk about environmental successes that we've done in a bipartisan way in the past because it shows that you can regulate environmental harm without destroying the economy.

I think it's partly because of inside-Washington politics that the environment has become a political football. Both sides make their reputations by sending their warriors out as gladiators in the fight about the environment versus jobs. It's useful for keeping the nation's politics polarized and so it keeps appearing really political, but I don't think in the end it really is, especially when you get down to the local level and start talking about the places that people really care about.

CB: How has the church gotten caught up in that? It seems like Christians may be even more fixated on the label issue.

RP: I wonder whether that is kind of a double diagnosis. Environmental issues in the secular world in the broader political public square have become politicized, and Christians have become more politicized. We tend to look at anything that is a conversation happening in the public square with our political lenses on. We think of ourselves as basically political animals. As much as we who are conservative Christians believe in small government, we do tend in a lot of instances to think that the way to solve some problems is to pass a law, and I think those conversations need to be happening somewhere else. We've kind of let the entertaining world of politics be the main arena for thinking about environmental action. That's just ridiculous.

CB: In what ways have we failed to understand what the issue really is?

RP: I think we have failed to consider the human face of the issue. The environment has been portrayed by its proponents as a sort of "protect the polar bears" movement. And environmentalists have not done a very good job of connecting environmental stewardship with caring for people. We've let secular environmentalism develop a reputation for caring more about animals than about people. One of the things that you get a good picture of when you talk to people on the mission field is the connection between environmental concerns and caring for people who need to make a living. I think Christians have got to really help to broaden that perspective. I've gotten in trouble before with environmentalists by saying, "I'm not an environmentalist." I think that dialogue has just gone too far down the road of being too political and too divorced from the welfare of people. The environmental conversation has left people out of it, in large measure.

CB: Shifting gears a little bit, what do you think the stewardship mandate is in terms of the everyday Christian who says, "Okay, I agree that God created the heavens and earth, and no, I'm not a fan of wrecked oil tankers, but is there really a stewardship mandate for me, and if so, what is it?"

RP: You can start by considering all of the proverbs that tell us about prudence, taking care of our families, making wise decisions, and being good stewards. There is an enlightened self-interest argument that you can get from the Bible, you can build out of the Christian virtues, where the end is really human welfare and the instrument for making that happen is a clean environment, a healthy living place.

But I think for a Christian, it goes deeper than that. The commands of Scripture given before the fall to tend and keep, to cultivate, to preserve and protect God's garden, and repeated after the fall in the covenant with Noah, show us that God has an ownership interest in the planet, and we have a stewardship responsibility. It's a feudal system. The ultimate Owner of all resources and property is the One who created it out of nothing—that's God. Because I can't do that, I only have a stewardship mandate to tend and keep, which means to preserve what's good and to restore what's broken—to bring shalom to broken places.

CB: At Flourish you talk about reviving lives and landscapes. That is a powerful visual for me in thinking about what you guys are about. What's the intersection there for you when you look at what's being done in the area of landscape revivals, whether it's urban renewal or massive projects in third-world countries where the environment has just been crushed?

RP: It's really hard for me to think about huge concepts like inhabiting the planet or being a global Christian in an ecological sense, but I can look out and see the houses and streets that people in my neighborhood inhabit. I look out right now and I see a day where there's a sort of gray haze outside. It started as a hot, clear summer day, but now it's one of those days when I need to tell the kids that they need to stay inside because the atmosphere is too risky for their young lungs. Conditions like this mean that kids who are on the verge of developing asthma are going to get worse and the kids that have asthma may end up in the emergency room. Those are things that are part of the landscape that are broken, where shalom doesn't exist, and I think it's really important for Christians to take responsibility for those places where they live and do what they can to restore them and make them healthy and good.

I want the kids in my neighborhood to develop a sense of Jehovah-Jireh, the One who can provide. They should get a sense of the attributes of God, His power, His divine nature, by looking at the creation, as Romans 1:20 says we should, but sometimes human action gets in the way of that. Reviving landscapes means bringing God's dominion and power back into those landscapes, making them healthy, and magnifying the witness of God.

CB: The classical argument against environmentalism and other efforts like this is that it is a distraction, that it is taking people away from the gospel. What would you say to that? It seems you're saying this isn't just environmentalism in the abstract. It's not "the most important thing you can do is save the polar bear" type of environmentalism.

RP: That's exactly right. It goes back to the Great Commission. We are to teach people. We are to proclaim to people what Jesus did, but also make disciples. We're to teach people to observe everything that God has commanded—going all the way back to the creation of the earth. By modeling that as the church, I think we give a really full view of what it is to become part of the body of Christ and to find yourself alive and renewed in that holy dominion that we're to exercise on the planet. I think of it as being faithful to the Great Commission—showing the world that we are actually serious about the commands of God and that it changes our lives in every way. It is far from a distraction.

CB: Is that taking root?

RP: Yes. I keep talking to pastors whose churches are beginning to take creation care seriously. They preach about it and are engaged in their community on it. They run outreach events that involve street cleanup and computer and cell phone recycling and at the same time explain what their church is doing and they find folks that have been long estranged from the church drawn to it. Over and over, there are stories of parents whose children come back to the church because now the church is showing itself to be interested in things that they, with the image of God in them, knew were right and good, but the churches had dismissed and they had never seen them recognized before by the church. It also causes us to get engaged in the world and in providing for the common good; we become salt and light in organizations that are not dominated by or originated by Christians.

CB: How do you dialogue with a pastor or perhaps the conservative elder who says, "Hey, it's great that we have all these new people at our church because they care about the environment, but are they also coming to terms with who Jesus is relationally to them?"

RP: There are a lot of people who are uncomfortable with the notion that Jesus is the only way to know God and they like the idea that you can be a Christian and be involved in other cultural projects that either leave the sharing of the gospel to other folks or just kind of leave it out altogether and make it very implicit. I worry about that.

Folks are involved in the creation care movement for all sorts of reasons, but I do meet people who are reluctant to talk about who Jesus is and what He did, and what His demands are on our lives, but that's been a problem even before there was any distraction from environmentalism. It's not a new thing that ordinary Christians in the pews don't really know how to share the gospel.

I think we're drifting in some ways into a "do good work, try to make a good reputation for the church" mentality, and hope that people figure out for themselves how to have a relationship with God.

We need to more clearly connect evangelism with environmental care. We do this because Jesus is Lord, because Jesus in His work on the cross has reconciled all things to Himself (Colossians 1). It's part of who we are as followers of Jesus, but we still need to be able to share the message of how we came to be followers of Jesus and invite others to be part of that project. It's a two-fold thing. We can make a connection with people, I think, because we ourselves bear the image of God, and that image is also alive in people with a concern for the environment. You can honor that, but you need to do the rest of the work—explaining why that image is in so many ways tarnished and broken and in need of restoration and that Jesus is the One who does that, who makes us truly able to be reconciled with God, ourselves, each other, and all of creation.

CB: The interesting thing is that we exist in the now but understand that there is something eternal going on.

RP: I think our position in this world right now is kind of like Israel in exile in Babylon (Jeremiah 29:4–14, especially v. 7) in which God commanded to build houses, settle down, plant gardens, eat what they produce, work for the peace of the city, work for the shalom of the city where you have been sent into exile, but know that I am going to restore you, restore the temple, bring people back, all the nations of the world will worship Me. You're in exile right now and you need to just be human while maintaining a witness for the gospel, for the Lord.

It's this planet that God has designed for us to live on. This is the planet that God will redeem and restore and us with it when He no longer subjects creation to futility. This is our home. We're made as creatures, physical creatures, and our existence in eternity is going to be as physical creatures in the image of God—what God always intended for it to be.

CB: That's a great point. It is really as simple as seeing how God uses His creation in my child's life. Every time my daughter spends time in Hawaii she matures in Christ. God touches her life and she grows in her understanding of God and His dominion over her and the world through walking on the beach, feeling the power of the waves, lying on the beach with turtles, and learning to experience the rain coming and going. If you get out in creation, He'll reveal Himself.

RP: I think connecting my kids to creation helps them to see God more clearly than plugging them into video games and whatever Hollywood is putting on the TV. It also makes them love and be concerned for the world that surrounds them. Because God is the creator, they see His work and admire His artistry, and know His birds by sight and by sound. They appreciate a lot about God from creation. I'm having to relearn and recultivate that in them and in me.

11

FRANCIS **CHAN**

Teaching Pastor, Cornerstone Church, Simi Valley, CA
Author of: *Crazy Love; Forgotten God*

It was a rainy morning as I started to drive from my home in San Diego to Francis Chan's church in Simi Valley, just north of Los Angeles. With just a tad over 150 miles to log, I had plenty of time to think about Francis and our discussion. A friend turned me on to him for this book, and to prepare I had purchased and read his two books and watched his video blogs. I was intrigued by his ideas, his church's commitment to give away 50 percent of their income, and the biblically solid messages preached in his books (which have sold well over five hundred thousand copies). I quickly realized that Chan was not another example of a now-tired genre—over-packaged "cool" pastors preaching soft theology in artistic ways. But I wanted to know why. I wanted to find out more about his personal journey and how he has handled the challenges of doing what this book suggests we all must.

Christian Buckley: In the preface to your book *Crazy Love*, you make the following statement:

173

God put me in Simi Valley, California, to lead a church of comfortable people into lives of risk and adventure. I believe He wants us to love others so much that we go to extremes to help them. I believe He wants us to be known for giving—of our time, our money, and our abilities—and to start a movement of "giving" churches. In so doing, we can alleviate the suffering in the world and change the reputation of His bride in America. Some people, even some at my church, have told me flat-out, "You're crazy." But I can't imagine devoting my life to a greater vision.

What triggered those perspectives?

Francis Chan: When it started, it took some faith in my personal life. I got to a point where I just knew God was going to provide because He showed me He would over and over again. I began to realize that the more we gave, the more we were fine. And after a while, it almost didn't feel like faith anymore because He'd shown me so many times. I got to the point that I just wasn't worried about myself. I'd tell my wife we could give everything away right then and it would work out. It's supernatural, God's watching. And He's shown us too many times.

So I had that personal conviction, but for some reason there was a block in my thinking because while I believed it for me, I didn't believe it for you. I knew God would take care of me, but I was scared to even ask people to give in case He wasn't going to come through for them like He did for me. I had to really think and ask myself, "Do I believe this for the sake of this church?" And I began to realize that I'm obviously not His favorite child, the only one He's going to do this for. He makes these promises in Scripture and I need to trust that the same principle that's been true in my life is true for all believers and true for the church at large.

As our church started to give more and more, it was overwhelming. It was like "tears-to-my-eyes" type of good. Our congregation just came alive. It was such a great change in our church, that my desire was for every church and Christian to experience it. It's just good.

CB: One of the things I find interesting in your process is where you started. You're a Masters Seminary graduate, right?

FC: Yes.

CB: So, I think the average person who knows the teaching of John MacArthur [founder and head of the Masters Seminary] would guess that a student of that school would be evangelically conservative, highly focused on Scripture, and very focused on the gospel, perhaps to the exclusion of humanitarian service and social justice. I would guess that the idea that we don't need to preach the gospel because "they will know we are Christians by our love" was not a favorite on that campus. I am not asking for a statement on MacArthur personally or the seminary specifically, but is that a fair characterization?

FC: It was true of my life. I don't want to make a general statement about other students or say that's the way it was for them, but it was true of me. And in reality my theology hasn't changed a ton as far as on paper, but it's this conviction to live it out. We had the orthodoxy, but maybe not the orthopraxy. In Scripture, it's one thing to declare who Jesus is and what He was like, but it's another thing to display what He was like. That's what I wasn't doing. All through Scripture, we're taught to walk as Jesus walked. That's as much a doctrine as teaching the way that He walked, and that was my big concern with the church—we've told people what Jesus was like, but we really didn't show it.

CB: So it is both?

FC: Scripture does emphasize both—watch your life and doctrine closely. If you do that, people are going to be saved. There's a power in that. But people neglect one or the other. Just doing a bunch of good stuff is not enough. Having your doctrine right-on is not enough. Your doctrine is not right-on until you're living it out.

Even now, I have to look at my life—like recently I confessed to the church on Sunday, I said, "I'm preaching grace, but I'm not living it. I haven't been showing grace to everyone I run into." And biblically, that's when you look at the role of an elder—it wasn't just to teach the right doctrine, but you really had to live it.

CB: It seems like we tend to be either/or type people. The last ten to fifteen years involved a "Christianity" defined by what we were against—a morality movement: we're anti-gay, we're anti-abortion, etc. And now we may be moving in a very different direction. It's almost a pendulum swing. Do you sense that?

FC: Absolutely, absolutely. I'm not a balance guy. I don't say, "Balance this, balance that." I see an extreme faith that we have. So I have to be hard-core defending doctrinally what I believe on paper, and I have to be hard-core living it out. It's not like, "Okay, balance the two of them." No. I want to know and be able to defend biblical truth and I've got to study and study hard, but I've also got to give and live and love with some desperation.

CB: You make the comment in *Crazy Love*, "The point of your life is to point to Him. Whatever you are doing, God wants to be glorified, because this whole thing is His. It is His movie, His world, His gift." And you talk in other places about the reality of how short and fragile our physical existence is. I take these comments to suggest a belief that what matters in the final sense is somebody's eternal status before God—are they forgiven, have they been reconciled?

At the same time, when you look at poverty, when you look at human trafficking, when you look at these great social evils that exist—that we walk in—they matter. They matter deeply to you and your church. So how do you confront both these issues? How do you say to the poor person, "Your poverty matters to me, but your soul matters more"?

FC: First, there are these tensions we have in our lives, like those you mentioned, that only the Holy Spirit can accomplish in us. For example, lately I've been wrestling with how to have great sorrow and unceasing anguish in my heart and at the same time rejoice always. I'm to always be rejoicing over my salvation and always anguishing over these people who are lost—bawling on this end and rejoicing on that end. How do I do that? Somehow it's got to be supernatural because on paper they seem mutually exclusive. I don't get it completely and that's where I go to the Holy Spirit and say, "Somehow these truths are in Scripture, and You need to make both of those things a reality in my life."

I would say the same is true in this instance. On the one hand I hurt for those in need. I wonder how I would feel if I were starving, if I couldn't find clean water for my family; what if I was being raped repeatedly all day, or my daughter was being raped repeatedly all day? On the other hand, there is a reality that, if that's anguish in this life, there's going to be even greater anguish afterward for those who don't know Him. There's an even bigger issue there.

Only the Holy Spirit at work in me can allow me to carry all of these burdens. I hate to be so simplistic, but I don't think you can write it out on paper. It's not going to work. It doesn't compute. It has to be supernatural because both are true and happening simultaneously. I have to look at that person as though it were Jesus. I've got to feed him, give him water, clothe him. At that same time I've got to deal with his eternal reality and need of the gospel.

CB: I don't like to live in a place where I realize it's going to be a day-by-day grind. I wish I could work out my Christianity so that it makes sense. So that there is nothing left for the Holy Spirit. I don't want to constantly look at that poor person in their poverty as both a spiritual and physical being because that's going to leave me without a comfortable resolution. What is it about us . . .

FC: I talk about that in *Forgotten God*. We're control freaks. We like to fix things, organize them. We don't like to follow. As a general rule, we like to be in control. I don't know if it's that we like to be in authority or that we want to know that we can package it and explain it and have it right there. Then we're sort of above the situation, we've got control of it versus just following, even though I don't know where I am going and why I'm going. We don't like that type of life where we just turn left here and trust that God is going to tell us where to go when we get to the end of the road. We say to God, "Why don't you just map everything out for me?"

CB: We do the same thing with the Word of God. You talk about it in the beginning of *Forgotten God*, that we don't go to the Scripture to really find out and do what it says. We want it to validate what we're doing. We don't adopt the position that whatever it says about an issue, that's what I'm going to do. It doesn't matter how I personally feel about it.

For example, it's easier to care about poverty than it is to care about people going to hell. And it's more popular. So is the answer to simply say, "What does the Scripture tell me and what is the Holy Spirit directing based on that?"

FC: It seems like it, it really does, but that doesn't leave you a whole lot of security for tomorrow outside of God. When Christ called His disciples, He was so clear with them: He was leading them into a life of uncertainty. Extreme uncertainty of not knowing what tomorrow was going to hold or even where they were going to sleep. So why should I believe that the Holy Spirit is going to do anything different in my life? I'm a very, very simple person. I wish I could grasp and memorize some of these deeper truths and be able to explain them, but the one thing the Lord has given me is clarity on the obvious and the simple and how we can distort it—not because it's confusing, but because we want to.

CB: You talk about that in the end of *Crazy Love*. You say the gap is so extreme in our world that we have to take lightly passages that challenge us to give and love radically. You are right. We don't take those passages seriously. You take them literally. You look at those passages and say, "I've got to do something with this literally in my life, in my church . . ."

FC: I was saying the other week that when I was a kid, it was really easy. Follow the leader—you did whatever the leader did. In church, "Follow Jesus" is a totally different game that we created. You can follow Him in your heart, but not in life. As a kid you can't just sit there and say, "I'm flapping my wings in my heart" rather than actually do what the leader was doing. Simon Says was really simple, you just did whatever Simon said to do. But Jesus Says is a totally different game in church. The way you play Jesus Says is you memorize what He said, you study what He said, and you quote what He said in the Greek; but you don't really have to do what He says. My head says it's simple—like childlike—you do what He did. You live how He lived. Certainly there is some thinking to do contextually and culturally—how does that look, and what's the best? But it's not going to look that different, it's not going to be that off—that whoever claims to live in Him must walk as Jesus walked. I see Scripture saying that over and over again. "Why do you call me Lord when you don't do what I say?" Those passages scream out to me. Jesus is stating very obviously, "Why do you call me Master if you're not going to obey me?" But we've created a system where you can call Him Master and not do what He says as long as you believe it in your heart. That doesn't compute with me. You can't just write these things off. They're very basic.

CB: That is not a popular idea. What has been the fallout for you?

FC: It's not taken well. There's a lot of resistance, but the reason why I have peace about continuing down this road is that the resistance I get is not with chapter and verse. People say things like, "God helps those who help themselves,"[5] my favorite "non-verse," and quote theories and Christian slogans we've created or verses like, "The ant saves and works hard."[6] They'll really twist Scripture; they'll say things like, "Jesus said you'll always have the poor," and argue that it means we shouldn't worry about them. Are you kidding me? Who's twisting the Scriptures here to get what they want? This is not what I want in the flesh. People say, "Oh, you don't like stuff, you don't love your kids, you don't want the best for them like I want for my kids." Their arguments are so off.

CB: You talk in the afterword to *Forgotten God* about the experience you had two years before the book came out, about going to a dinner and sitting next to somebody who was involved in the human trafficking issue. The passion you felt and how that was numbed by other well-meaning Christians. Talk about that.

FC: It was such a process. It was David Batstone, by the way, from Not For Sale. He didn't even talk about it a whole lot. When I went back to the hotel and tried to dwell on the few things he did say, and just the concept of it—when I put a face to it and thought of my own daughters, I came home and wanted to really get involved in the issue.

What I got was the typical American church response. Don't get me wrong, there are plenty of people here that are hard core—heart's broken, and doing things about it. We've got people going back and forth to Thailand. But the general populace is never going to go for that. And I started listening, listening, listening, and I've got temptations myself and so many distractions. That's my biggest weakness. I love to play anything. My perfect day is wake up, surf, golf, have dinner with my wife and a bunch of friends —a great day. So that temptation is there. When people say, "Settle down, let's go do this, let's go do that," I jump right back into that world. I'm no saint who's gotten rid of all these fleshly passions. It's all there. I'm going to gravitate toward that unless I really fast and pray and seek the Spirit and ask, "What do You want me to do right now?"

It's the sick side of us that doesn't want anyone to be too radical. It's convicting. People make these statements like, "You're a radical. God doesn't call us all to be that way. Listen Francis, you have this weird idea that there's this little group of radicals and that they're the real believers; you know, there's a middle of the road too. There's this middle road where people do good things." I see a narrow road and a wide road. That's all I read about.

CB: Picking up on that last idea. It really personalizes God's call in your life. What is the difference in your mind between focusing on individuals rather than focusing on institutions or issues?

FC: It's interesting that I was never motivated, sadly, by the issue of poverty. It wasn't until I became friends with people and I started interacting with individuals in Africa, and there was a face to it—that's when everything changed for me. It was that personal side. At least that brought it to light, and now I have these people in mind, these faces I saw, and these conversations we had, and suddenly it was my friend who was starving, and she has a name that no one takes the time to get to know, but she does. It's interesting that it was never an issue because I separated myself from the issue, but I couldn't separate myself from those individuals, looking into their eyes.

12

BRAD **CORRIGAN**

Founder and President, Love Light & Melody

Brad Corrigan is a rock star in sheep's clothing. His former band, Dispatch, sold out three nights at Madison Square Garden in 2006 and played a farewell show to one hundred thousand–plus fans just a couple of years before that. But if you met Brad and didn't know about Dispatch (as I didn't), you would never know any of that. I first got to know Brad at least five years ago, and while our paths rarely cross, I am always grateful when they do. Brad left Dispatch to do something else, something that God was trying to show him. As it turns out, he found that something in a trash dump in Nicaragua. Through Love Light & Melody, Brad and his friends are bringing something new to what he calls his family. It is a different kind of humanitarian work, but you can't miss the impact it has on the people of that dump, or on Brad.

Each year they perform a concert, the *Dia de Luz*, in the middle of the trash dump, as an expression of their mission. In their words, they are "committed to becoming experts on the life and culture inside the city trash dump in Managua, Nicaragua. Our goal is to identify and meet the immediate physical needs, raise awareness about trash dump communities, and fight social injustice. We use music and the arts to rebuild, restore, and bring healing to communities ravaged by extreme poverty."

I attended Not For Sale's Global Forum on Human Trafficking to see Brad and several other well-known artists, including Foreman of Switchfoot, perform a benefit concert. What started as a crossing of paths turned into a conversation and ended at my house late that night, us strumming ukuleles and talking about Brad's work. Fortunately, I was able to record his words from the stage during his set.

DURING CONCERT, CARLSBAD, CALIFORNIA, 7:33 PM

So I feel like this is a unique time for us as musicians to be completely free. For this is why we play. We don't play to sell CDs and we don't play to sell tickets. And that's what the modern day has done: to hijack and take captive the musicians that have been trying for so long to be able to speak, sing, bring melodies and beats that are about a new way and about setting people free. So when I look up and see the eyes of these kids it reminds me so much of the kids that God's used to wreck my heart in the most beautiful way. And they're scattered all over creation and they all have the same beauty in their eyes and in their smile and that is why we sing. It is a joy to make music for them, it is a joy to make music for Him, it is a joy to make music tonight.

This is a song called "Ileana" . . . it is about a thirteen-year-old girl who is now sixteen. I met her in a trash dump in Central America where she lives and works. Her primary means of making money for her family was to be a prostitute. She started when she was eight. And she is the most precious and gorgeous thing you have ever ever seen. I wrote in my journal that she was like finding a white rose in a war zone. So this song is real, this song is about a girl that I feel like is my daughter, that I would do anything for, so I bring her here for you now . . .

You may not know their names, you may not know where they're from. But the beautiful simplicity is that they are family, or at least we can choose to see them that way. We can also see them as strangers and walk away. But those are really your only two choices—see them as family and then what would you not do, or see them as strangers, which means they'll probably look back at you as just the same. It really is just a process of deciding that they are family. I didn't mean to, but a little girl in a trash dump in Central America has given me everything. God has used a little girl in a trash dump, a place where they have less than our definition of nothing—they are living in what we have discarded. How is it that my fam-ily in a trash dump has taught me what it means to be generous? How is it that people who have nothing to give, have out-given me?

When you walk with people who are smiling and laughing in the midst of a hell like that . . . you will say . . . "How could I possibly want . . . ?"

ON THE DRIVE HOME, 10:32 PM

Christian Buckley: What is Love Light & Melody?

Brad Corrigan: In large part we are a collective of storytellers trying to raise awareness and create actionable steps. We are trying to carry God's sto-ries of redemption in a very unique way. We are trying our hardest not to get in the way.

Love Light & Melody is about our core values of how change happens in your own heart—not to feel guilty, but to feel empowered to use the gifts that you have for others. The point is connecting people who are stirred by what we do in the storytelling to brick-and-mortar organizations that are in the dump. We are just trying to draw people together to work with what is going on down there. We are also trying to get the organizations to work together. We tell a story, and then we want to connect people to it.

CB: What was the moment for you that you felt God saying, "I have this for you"?

BC: I played a little fund-raiser in Virginia Beach for an orphanage in Nicaragua. I said, "I love kids, I'll do it." I got an invitation that same month to play a youth rally in Nicaragua, and I said, "What is going on with me and Nicaragua?" So I went and did the youth rally, and then this taxi driver, Biz-mark, saw I had a heart for kids and he took me on a tour of the city because he had a ministry to street kids. He is now one of my best friends.

So he took me into the dump, and I thought we were going in the wrong direction. It looks and feels and smells like a war zone—there is nothing good about it. Smoke and fire and all kinds of chaos. All of a sudden through the smoke I see roof lines and kids playing soccer. The Lord really communicated it to me in that very first trip that my heart was there. But I went there ten times that year and never got out of the taxi once. I was so afraid. It was really intimidating. I would go in, cry, take pictures, and leave—fifteen minutes, max. I would go to the orphanage, but before I left I would always ask Bizmark to take me back, take me back, take me back. And then on the eleventh or twelfth time, this little girl (Ileana) knocked on the taxi window, introduced herself, and pulled me out of the car. She was so excited to show me her home and her parents. She was so strong, just incredible . . .

CB: That must have really impacted you.

BC: The most transformational stuff that has happened in my life has been taught in that trash dump through these precious kids and families and how I have received the Lord's love through them. It has been just nearly beyond description.

SAN DIEGO, MY LIVING ROOM, 11:45 PM

CB: You didn't find a cause, it found you. What allowed that to happen in your heart?

BC: I think you just have to journey out and follow Jesus. It's about following Him and having the courage to go where He went and love people the way He loved people—you start walking in the Lord's power.

I had traveled all over the world and passed by countless social injustices. I wasn't looking for one, but the Lord just planted me there. There was no question. Something was different that day. This girl got my heart. These kids and these families have my heart.

You know, but you have to say, "Here am I." I think the only thing I have ever done in my part of the equation was to say, "I'll go." I don't know what we are going to do there. But it really just takes a child's faith to say, "I am available."

CB: It took a kid to knock on your door. God sent a child to get you out of the cab.

BC: God was saying, "Look at the strength in her, Brad. She's not afraid out there. If she has the ability to laugh over this tragedy, I will give you the power to do the same."

CB: So you have played three March concerts in the dump, Dia de Luz, in 2007, 2008, and 2009. And you have played in front of one hundred thousand people in America. Can you compare the two?

BC: The comparison? Oh gosh . . . it's wild. But I'll tell you where the gift of music comes alive is in the trash dump, more than any other place, because it's like bringing someone cool water who's been thirsty for days. It's like bringing someone a dream who has just been struggling with nightmares for so long. They close their eyes, they dance, they sing, they clap, they escape. You see music's purest power when people who don't ever really get to listen to it are standing in the midst of it.

I think the craziest juxtaposition for me was three nights of sold-out Madison Square Garden, and then a couple months later to be in the trash dump. To just go, "You know, that was really fun back there at MSG, but these people here, when I play music here, it is life-giving. It is not entertainment, it is absolutely life-giving."

CB: Do you feel like when you play music, when you use your craft and creative power, do you feel like the people who are hearing your music are experiencing God's power in that creative moment?

BC: Oh yeah, I think so. We are all made in His image and when He breathed His creation into existence, it was the most pure harmony that's ever existed. We've brought dissonance into His harmonically perfect thing. I feel like music is the Lord's breath when you give it to Him. There is healing and tears and joy. There is so much power in it.

CB: Does it matter whether you are working with a Christian group or a secular group in what you are doing?

BC: I think the heartbeat of Jesus is the most powerful thing. Following the Man and seeing how His heart broke. You have to see what broke His heart. You have to follow Him.

But if there's not excellence first, it doesn't matter whether you're Christian or not. Your work has to be excellent. You've got to have a track record that shows that this is more than something that is convenient. It's more than a phase. It's sacrificial—that even on days that I don't feel like it, I am going to live for this person because they are family. I think once you establish that, you are the real deal; people are going to ask what you believe in—what is behind it.

CB: I think it is interesting that you look at what you are doing as working with family.

BC: It's not a cause. If you look at people as a cause, I think you miss the most significant part of the equation. They are your family. We don't ever want to impose ourselves. We want to love people and share life with them. We want to tell stories out of that life. You can't fast forward that. When you look at people as your family it totally changes everything.

CB: You really look at the world differently. You don't look at issues and problems.

BC: If you do that, you miss the people right under your nose. You also can miss the point of really considering what poverty is. I can see "poor" people who have heart wealth and "rich" people who have nothing. We really need to take a closer look at what spiritual wealth and poverty is. We need to go and listen.

13

ISAAC **SHAW**

Executive Director, Delhi Bible Institute

Isaac Shaw is the executive director of Delhi Bible Institute (DBI), an organization that has been training church leaders at all levels and planting them in churches all over India for more than fifty years. Their current vision is to train thirty thousand students and plant fifteen thousand new Bible-preaching churches throughout North India by the year 2025—all in the midst of abject poverty. Their goal isn't social, but that isn't because Isaac doesn't understand poverty—he grew up in it.

Christian Buckley: Talk about the plight of Northern India.

Isaac Shaw: Well, in round numbers, India is 1.2 billion people. Eighty percent of them are Hindus, 13 percent of them are Muslims, and 2.4 percent of them are Christians. Northern India is about six hundred million people and is the birthplace of Hinduism, Sikhism, Jainism, and Buddhism. Northern India is also very critical because 90 percent of all Christians that live in India live outside of Northern India, and only 10 percent of Christians live in Northern India. So where 50 percent of the population is, 10 percent of the Christians are there. And at the most basic level, only 2 percent of the 2.4 percent who are labeled as Christians in all of India actually believe the Bible as we do.

CB: How does poverty play into that?

IS: If you take the 1.2 billion people, eight hundred million of these live on less than a dollar a day salary, and four hundred million of them live below the bread line—they eat once in forty-eight hours.

CB: Did that impact you growing up in India?

IS: When I was three, I lost my mother. I was abandoned in a city of eighteen million people. I remember one day I was so hungry, and there was no food that I ate a newspaper. I ate a newspaper. That is part of my identity because I know what it means to be hungry, I know what it means to be poor, and I know what it means not to have anything. The first time I visited the West, a food store in the West, I passed out in the food store. I passed out. I was unconscious in the food store because I had never seen so much food in my life.

I bear the scars of that childhood. But I can tell you that only in Christ Jesus can you take a disadvantage, turn it into an advantage, and use it for the glory of God. I have a heart for the poor because I was poor. I was rescued by a man who rescued me because his heart was transformed by the gospel.

CB: So how do you view poverty now, and what is the solution?

IS: Today, you know that the transformational impact of the gospel in my life has just radically altered my worldview. I tell you that human suffering is just one more statement that governs my outlook. When we look at human suffering, we react; we don't respond. And we reactively want to do things. And most of the time that does not help. But let me tell you God's solution. There is only one religion in the world where there is a cross and there is a Savior. Where there is suffering and there is somebody who brings you out of that suffering. And if we don't have that right, we'll keep react-ing, not responding. We will bring bread, but we will not bring the Bread of Life to the people.

CB: Talk more about that. In what ways do you believe we have reacted poorly?

IS: As soon as the church looks at India, they get involved in the social gospel. That is the default mode. In my twenty-seven years of experience in the mission's world in India, I have been associated with many people who did both things. Some of them did just the social gospel and others did preaching of the Word. I don't think in many instances we asked what India really needed. For example, in the past, many Christian hospitals and schools were opened and we now have generations of people, Hindus and Muslims alike, who have benefited from these institutions. But in 2008, 2009, and the last ten years, when the church has been persecuted severely, the people who benefited from the Christian institutions remained quiet. So while we did good works, which we should as Christians, what has been the benefit to the church? And the church has remained as weak as it was, and these peo-ple have just looked on and in fact have developed strong biases against the church.

CB: So when the church—for sake of discussion let's call it the Western church—looked on at India and the poverty, the reaction was to create Christian organizations to do work, but for many of the people who have come through those organizations—been raised in them—there has in fact been no true Christianity that's been imparted to them.

IS: I believe the problem that is there is that all these institutions are paral-lel to the church or outside the church or remotely associated with the church. They are run by Christians, but they are not linked to the church, they are not under the church, they have not been appointed by the church. The issue is not just reacting, but finding a way to respond that puts God in the middle of all of this.

Early on I went into one poor community and they said they needed help, and of course they did need it. So we provided them food, shelter, clothing; we taught them Christian songs; we taught them to celebrate Christmas and Easter; and we had a group of people who could sing Christian songs, who knew what Christmas and Easter were, who prayed and had Bibles—but were they a transformed community? They were not. Why? Because help came before the gospel. Was that model successful? It wasn't successful for us.

What I believe is that instead of doing this, God's solution for poverty and other social issues in India is the church. Let us not put church as second rate to social work. And I'm talking about the very basics of church—the Word of God is faithfully proclaimed, there is discipline, and there are sacraments.

CB: So the solution to poverty in your opinion is not going to come from international social investment?

IS: I believe the solution for poverty is not social work; the solution for poverty is a living church. It's a group of transformed believers from [whom] heart selfishness and self-centeredness has been locked out and has been replaced by the love of people and love for the poor. That community goes out and works on the transformation of the people, not just changing their condition by helping, but changing their heart from inside. For us, churches are going to be centers for helping the poor through the gospel, through their lives being transformed. We have a social and relief initiative at DBI, but it is important where and when it comes.

CB: Okay. So how should the Western church give? How do we engage?

IS: I think giving needs to be strategic—even for the poor. When I was talking about the four hundred million poor people, you can take a jumbo jet with dollar bills and shower it over Northern India every day, and after a year you can land your jumbo jet and go and see whether you changed the plight of anyone. You didn't, because I believe poverty has to be dealt with relationally, not reactively. Disasters can be handled reactively because you need a front line and aid to help people immediately. But poverty has to be tackled on a long-term basis. That's why we believe that permanent communities have to be there on the ground so that there can be long-term interaction and relation with the poor rather than just throwing money at the poor. We need to have a strategy of getting alongside the local church in the local community and coming alongside and helping them.

CB: What do you think Christ meant when He said the poor will always be with us?

IS: You know, people sometimes say I am anti-poor, that I don't want to help the poor because of my views. You are talking to a man who all his life has helped the poor. On my children's birthdays, we go and help the poor; every one of my children, we have taught them. I have given radical notes as gifts to people, and I have said, "Today at your wedding, five hundred people were fed here, and I fed five hundred people more in the slums as a wedding gift on your wedding." I have done radical things like that, but when I talk about it, where my theology is behind that is very, very clear. See, one side is, "What does it profit a man if he gains the whole world and loses his whole soul?" One is the rich man's half of it—what will it profit? The other side is that beggar Lazarus in front of the home of that rich man. And what was the escape of the beggar was knowing his destiny. I think the effort that the church has spent in improving the situation of people in the world and not being able to change their spiritual situation, or not addressing that need in many ways, exemplifies where the church is in this century—concerned more about its image rather than about its message of eternal life.

CB: So in conclusion, what I hear you saying is that in your experience in India over the last twenty-seven years, charity has come without redemption—it comes and it goes and it cannot be sustained. It can only be sustained through a growing, living Bible church in a community that sustains that radical change.

IS: Absolutely. Help will not transform lives. Do you know a rich man is as selfish as a poor man? And a poor man is as selfish as a rich man? You know, we have the story of these two men sitting under the tree. They both were hungry, they both were homeless, they both had not eaten in a long time, and they both prayed and said, "God, please give us food from the sky." Bread fell into the lap of one of them and he got up with the bread and left, saying to the other guy, "I wonder why God has not heard your prayer." The poor man is as selfish as the rich man. The issue is bigger than poverty. The issue of transformation is much, much bigger than poverty, and unless we address that issue, we're just putting a Band-Aid on the whole issue. We're just saying we will not deal with the cause. The cause is the human heart because the human heart is desperately wicked. India produces enough food to feed all its people. India manufactures enough clothing to clothe all its people. Then why are there poor and why are there naked people? Why? Because the whole system is corrupted by hearts that have not been transformed.

14

BRYAN **KEMPER**

Founder and President, Stand True Ministries
Author of *Social Justice Begins in the Womb*

M any pro-life activists today seek to change hearts, minds, and policies through quiet, behind-the-scenes work—and then there's Bryan Kemper. The founder of Stand True and Rock for Life, Kemper prefers a more—*ahem*—direct approach. His in-your-face passion for the unborn is certainly provocative, but as he argues in a new book, abortion may be among the most important humanitarian causes God's people can adopt. The author of *Social Justice Begins in the Womb* held nothing back in this wide-ranging interview.

Ryan Dobson: Talk about your history in the pro-life movement and the first organization that you founded, Rock for Life, and then let's get into your breaking apart from that ministry and starting Stand True.

Bryan Kemper: Absolutely. For me, it's about human personhood. It's about standing up for our fellow human person. You know, Christ says that the two greatest things are to love your God with all your heart, soul, and your mind, and to love your neighbor as yourself. And for me, the reason I got into pro-life work and founded Rock for Life and now Stand True, is because I believe that every child in the womb is our neighbor. That every single human person on the face of this earth is our neighbor. Our neighbor is not just the guy next door who won't return your hammer. Our neighbor is our fellow human person. And for so many years now, you know, four thousand of our neighbors are killed every single day in the name of choice through surgical abortion. And so in 1993 I started Rock for Life as sort of an answer for the youth to get involved in pro-life. There was really no youth pro-life movement at that time. And I worked with some great Christian bands, and we just started doing concerts, and I toured with Lollapalooza. And it turned into one of the largest youth pro-life organizations in the world.

Then about six years ago, I founded Stand True. For me, I really wanted to bring the gospel of Christ back to the center of the pro-life movement. And I felt that we needed to really be a loving, compassionate, good, Christ-centered pro-life movement, and not just the angry anti-abortion movement of the '80s and '90s. In fact, then it was really a lot of in-your-face and protests and that kind of stuff, and that was kind of the culture back then. But now I believe we really need to bring this into a Christ-centered, loving, compassionate, pro-life movement. So I started Stand True with that in mind.

RD: So did it feel early on like an "us vs. them," and now it's more "we're in this together," where you're trying to have that conversation?

BK: Yeah, I think at first it was sort of like you had to have some kind of ignition—something that really sparked the debate. And you know, I was involved in a lot of the protests, and I think that there was a lot of good stuff that went on back then. You know, it was simple disobedience that was done in a very peaceful, loving way—similar to Martin Luther King Jr. sitting at the lunch counters. We would just sit down and pray in front of the abortion mills, and I had been arrested several times for simply praying. But obviously now with all the federal laws things have changed; you really can't do that anymore.

Now for us, it's about engaging this culture and engaging this generation in conversation and educating people. With all the technology that we have today, with the 3D and 4D ultrasounds and all of the life development facts that we have. And just the advances in medicine and seeing that picture of that little baby that was being operated on while still in the womb—you remember that picture, where it reached out and grabbed the doctor's fingers?

RD: Yeah.

BK: With all of that stuff we have now, it's all about conversation. You can just use that to logically show people where life begins. I think it's so much more effective when we're out there engaging the culture, engaging this generation, and then turning it on to Christ.

RD: Yes, definitely. You talked about bringing Jesus Christ back into the movement. Explain that more in depth.

BK: So many times I hear organizations say we just need to leave Jesus out of it. We just need to go scientifically, we just need to do this, we just need to do that. We've got to overturn *Roe v. Wade*. And if you really look at how we're going to end abortion in this country, overturning *Roe v. Wade*, while that would be a great step, it's not the end-all.

In fact, all that would do is turn abortion laws right back to the states. And with the first state that tried to stop it, it would go right back to court, to federal court, back to the Supreme Court for another decision. There is only one true political answer to ending abortion in America, and that is through a paramount human life amendment to the constitution, declaring that every single human person from the moment of fertilization to natural death is a full human person. And the only way to do that is by turning hearts to Christ. That's truly the only way we're going to do that. And to show that a full human person means that a person has a soul—that person was created by God with a purpose. And so, if Christ is left out, we cannot win this battle.

RD: You know, it's interesting, I was up at North Shore Christian Fellowship Church on Sunday and the pastor said that exact thing: If you want to end the abortion debate, talk about the soul. When does the soul enter our body? It enters at fertilization. That means it's a person. And it really becomes a spiritual issue, not a scientific issue.

BK: Well, look what happens when we separate science from God. You get freaky, Frankenstein science, like embryonic stem cell research and all this stuff. The fact is, science is not true without God. And so, yeah, you have to have the gospel as a part of that. And the fact that God is the creator of every life, that God is the one who gives us a soul, and that we don't have the right to take away and harm human life.

RD: Talk about the gospel in the work that you do. How is the gospel utilized in the work that you're doing with Stand True?

BK: Well, we take so many different ways of trying to get the message out. We try to use a lot of new media—Facebook, MySpace. Even as simple as the T-shirts that we print. For years, you probably remember the big, bold, screaming in your face, "Abortion is murder," "Abortion is homicide"—all these T-shirts that were just screaming in your face. And you couldn't walk around a Christian festival without seeing that every other foot.

We're trying to use artwork and use creativity to spread the gospel and spread the pro-life message in a way that's more subtle, more creative, that's thought-provoking and asks questions. If you're going to wear one of our T-shirts, when people ask you, "Hey what does that mean exactly?" it gives you the opportunity to share the gospel, to share the pro-life message with people. In the new book I've written, *Social Justice Begins in the Womb*, I talk about a lot of this stuff, about how we need to have the gospel as the center of our lives and go get out there.

Even in the ministry, when we go out, and you minister to people about abortion, it's probably one of the darkest and most oppressive subjects there is. People don't like to talk about it. And it can really be a bummer. So if you're not at a place in your life, if you're not prayed up, if you're not really grounded in the Word, you're going to have a hard time doing it.

So with us, we try to encourage kids—we take kids out on our summer mission trip, and we really build them up in the pro-life message, but also in living their lives everyday for Christ. Not knowing what tomorrow brings, we're not promised tomorrow. So every day our lives need to be centered on Christ. And looking for those opportunities for God to open up and talk to them, especially when it comes to post-abortion healing. When you have women who are hurt, who are just wrecked inside when they realize what they've done, there is only one thing that can fix that, and that's the hope of Christ.

RD: Brian, talk about the church. I'm not a church basher, but talk about the way the church has missed the issue with the gospel and the unborn. There are good things happening in the church, but there are ways that maybe in the past, they kind of missed it. You know, the guns pointed outward, instead of arms opened up.

BK: Well, it's interesting because I think that for the most part, the church has sort of treated abortion as a political issue. It's kind of left it up to each election cycle. Every time there is a new presidential election, people start talking about abortion again, and they seem to think as long as we elect the right president, then we've done our part, and we've battled it the right way. And that's something I've just avoided, because I don't see that as the key issue here. The fact is, as you and I have said, it's a gospel issue. It's more of a spiritual issue, and we need to be reaching out to people. And I think that people get involved in pro-life, and they fade away very fast. One, because it is so oppressive. It's not a pleasant thing. It's not something that people like to talk about. You don't want to think about dead babies.

And another reason I think is because you don't always see the results right away. You know, you've probably gone to a soup kitchen, and when you hand that homeless guy that bowl of hot stew, you feel good about what you've just done. You see his face light up. You see him sit down and start to eat, and his cheeks get warm. And you get those, like, Holy Spirit goosebumps, because you feel good about seeing the results of the work that you just did.

So when it comes to pro-life work, a lot of times, you don't get to see the results. You're out there talking to people and you may never see the results. And so it can be very frustrating, and I think that's the reason that we've seen some of the upsurge, the more violent tactics, and some of the screaming and the yelling. People have taken things into their own hands, matters into their own hands, because they're not seeing the results. And we just need to do the work and understand that God's in charge of the results, not us. I have never saved a single baby's life. Stand True has never saved a single baby's life—only God has. And that's the way we have to look at it.

RD: How do you not get jaded? Going through the situation where you see and understand there's four thousand babies a day being killed. How do you continue on with hope or with a positive attitude or with the desire to have a conversation and not get angry?

BK: I'll tell you, I think God has continued to give me grace, and continued to give me events in my life that have sort of renewed me or reenergized me or helped me to continue. I went in March to Auschwitz in Poland. And as I walked through this concentration camp, and I saw things like the room of hair that they took off the Jews, and made blankets and jackets for the Nazi soldiers out of the Jews' hair. I saw this little pair of hand-knit, wool baby's pants that looked exactly like the wool pants we put on my little boy over his cloth diapers, and I just started bawling my eyes out as I was seeing this. And then we went and saw the rubble of the building where they incinerated human beings. Where they took grandmas and grandpas and little baby boys and girls and people and told them they're about to get a shower because they had just ridden in a train for six or seven days, standing up, with no sanitation. And then they gassed them to death.

And as I was looking at this building, I saw some houses in the distance. These were houses that were there when this building was in operation. And

I was thinking to myself, "What if that was my house? What if I had lived there during the time of this concentration camp? What if I had come out of my back door one day, having a cup of coffee, with my kids playing in the yard, and I saw that incinerator, and I saw those ashes flying through the air, and I saw those people being marched into that building, but never coming out? What would I have done? Would I have stood up? Would I have been a voice? Or would I have ignored it and just watched my fellow human person die in that concentration camp?" And I was thinking about this, and I realized that that *is* my house. We do live there, because we live in a country where there are buildings all over this nation where little baby boys and girls go in every day alive with a heartbeat, with blood pumping through their veins, but they never come out alive. And I see things like that, and it motivates me to continue on. As long as I know that that is happening every day in my country, every day in this world, then I must stand up. I have to be a voice. How can I not stand up and be a voice?

RD: Bryan, tell us something about the ministry that you do that we don't know about. You know, maybe something behind the scenes or something people have misconstrued. Who is it that you are, internally, that we don't know?

BK: You know, I'm really just this nerd. I sometimes ask myself, "God, why me? Why pick me?" I'm a high school dropout. I'm a former drug dealer. I come from one of the worst backgrounds that you could come from. Yet God has used me to do this work. And so I only can rely on Christ. And this ministry, you know, we scrape by, by the skin of our teeth, like so many people, but God always provides. And we're just out there.

Whenever I give a pro-life talk at a conference, I start with my testimony about coming to Christ, because I couldn't do anything in my life if it weren't for Christ. It's not even possible to do this interview, to be able to do anything. I don't deserve anything on my own but death, except that Christ died for me.

15

MIKE **YANKOSKI**

Community Member, The Ranch

Author of *Under the Overpass; Zealous Love*

Mike Yankoski's unorthodox 2004 "pilgrimage" left out Rome, Constantinople, Jerusalem—and every other historic Christian site. Instead, he spent six months sleeping under bridges and eating at street kitchens in six large American cities. Mike and his friend Sam Purvis emerged from their homelessness journey physically unscathed but spiritually pierced with an enduring desire to minister to the world's hurting and needy. Now a graduate student at Regent College in Canada, Mike and his wife, Danae, the coauthor of Francis Chan's bestsellers, live in a Co:Here community house in Vancouver's Downtown Eastside.

Ryan Dobson: Mike, tell me about *Under the Overpass* and your call into homelessness and the homeless ministry.

Mike Yankoski: As you know, Sam and I were on the streets about six years ago—actually it was 2004, and *Under the Overpass* came out in 2005. So for the past five years now I've been traveling and speaking about caring for the homeless, and this has taken an interesting turn. My wife, Danae, and I are actually living in a community house now in Vancouver's Downtown Eastside, which is the tougher area of Vancouver. The whole vision of the community house is to provide long-term living situations for people who are vulnerable or who have barriers to living on their own. We also have a short-term apartment that's used for people who are coming straight off the streets, for them to be able to get in out of the elements for a little while. They can join in with the life and rhythms of the community as they want to.

There's a gentleman from Iraq, a refugee because of some of the things that Saddam Hussein did to the Kurdish people in the northern regions of Iraq, who fled from Iran and came to Canada. He lives in the community house and has been here for six years. Another guy who has been recovering from pretty heavy drug and alcohol addictions is living here as well and has been clean for three years. He is finding in community a really strong way for him to continue on the path toward becoming who he's supposed to be.

We're trying to live into some of these things, because one of the biggest frustrations that Sam and I had as we were on the streets was the question of why Christians aren't being what they claim to be. Why aren't people loving unconditionally? Oftentimes you walk into a church and you feel very conditional love—you have to look a certain way, you have to dress a certain way, smell a certain way, you have to make a certain amount of money, drive a certain kind of car, live in a certain kind of house, have a certain kind of resume, whatever, in order to be accepted and in order to be loved. That's clearly not what's going on in the Gospels.

As we read the Scriptures and as we see what Jesus is doing, He's loving the people who those in positions of influence and power—like the Roman government, the Pharisees, and the Jewish hierarchical system—had cast out. He's hanging out with the prostitutes, tax collectors, and lepers who are societal outcasts. He spends more time with outcasts than He does with people in the "in crowd." What does that mean for us today as Christians? That is a big question that Danae and I have been trying to figure out, and specifically a big question that we're trying to live into by being in the community house. One of my biggest frustrations that led to the whole journey of living on the streets for those five months with Sam was the realization that, man, I'm talking about this Christian faith, but I'm not actually living it out; I'm not actually doing anything with it. It's just talk, it's just words.

Theologically one of my core convictions comes from 1 John 4:19, where John summarizes the Law and the commandments as Jesus had done, and then he says, "We love because he first loved us." So we are loved by God—by the Creator God, by our Father and by His Son, Jesus Christ—and therefore we ought to love others. That's the linking together that Jesus did when He answered the question, "What is *the* great commandment?" He gave a double answer. He said, "Love the Lord your God with all your heart, all your mind, all your soul, all your strength" *and* "Love your neighbor as yourself." Those two things are combined, so it's both about our vertical, personal relationship with God and our horizontal, interpersonal relationships with the people around us.

You look at Jesus touching the leper. Well, in that society, you just didn't do that—when you touched a leper in Jesus' day, you become unclean. Well, Jesus is completely reversing this, stretching across that societal boundary, touching the leper and healing him. This is the model that we see in Jesus Christ and in how He related to outcasts, how He related to the poor, to the people that nobody else wanted to be around. He was building relationships with them, counting them among His friends. He was eating meals with them, being associated with them.

Those are some of the big questions that Danae and I have been asking the past few years. And that has led us into our new book project, *Zealous Love*, which takes eight major areas of need in our world, eight major areas that impact billions of people, and asks, "What does it mean to love our neighbors as ourselves given these great needs?"

RD: List those eight areas, and then talk about how we live out the gospel in relation to them.

MY: The first one is human trafficking. The second is unclean water. Third, refugees. Fourth, hunger. Fifth, lack of education. Sixth, creation degradation. Seventh, HIV and AIDS. And eighth, economic inequality. We asked people who have been working in those areas to reflect on their work, so the book is very story based. We wrote the introductions to each of those sections and asked people to share their stories and experiences.

We start off in *Zealous Love* thinking about that 1 John 4:19 passage and about Philippians 2:3–4, where Paul says, "Do nothing from rivalry or vain conceit but instead consider others more significant than yourselves. Let each of you be ready to look not only to your own interests but also to the interests of others." And to think about loving our neighbors as ourselves, and in Matthew 25 caring for the least of these, in the context of all of these great needs. To summarize what *Zealous Love* is all about, it's first about becoming mindful of the reality of our world.

It's much more comfortable to exist in our own sort of bubble, to be myopic and selfish and inwardly focused. So we don't really know what's going on in our world; we don't take the time to dig into the facts and to find out exactly what's going on for people who live halfway around the world. But that information is available. More and more people are becoming knowledgeable about the fact that, for example, somewhere between twelve and twenty-seven million people are enslaved today. Well, what does it mean to love your neighbor as yourself when you know that there are still slaves? We think about Jesus saying, "I have come to set the captives free."

RD: Mike, you lived in the homeless community for five months, you've written an amazing book on it, and now you're speaking about *Zealous Love*. Some people would say, "Mike, that's amazing, but all you're doing is saving the body and not the soul." Playing devil's advocate, at what point does the gospel meet the road in saving the soul with the body?

MY: This comes down to core theology. Who do we understand God to be? Who do we understand ourselves to be? And what do we understand our task on this earth to be? As I have begun to read and think and learn a lot more about this, I've come to think it's a false dichotomy to say, "Should I love someone by feeding them?" or "Should I love someone by preaching the gospel to them?" We've divided those two things, but I think as we read the Scriptures we see that Jesus is both healing people and proclaiming the coming kingdom of God. He's proclaiming the coming kingdom of God by feeding people. He's proclaiming the coming kingdom of God by convicting people of their sin. He's proclaiming the coming kingdom of God by living the coming kingdom of God. So when we start to ask questions like, "Should we save someone from slavery, or should we tell them about Jesus Christ?" I think we're making a mistake. To live the gospel is to free someone from slavery and in so doing to proclaim Jesus Christ as the Lord and Savior of all humankind—as the one who comes to liberate us both from our physical slavery, from our slavery that's interpersonal, societal, and systemic, as well as our individual and spiritual slavery to sin. Both of these things are going on.

I think sometimes, unfortunately, we over-spiritualize the gospel and think that it's only about the spiritual realm. I want to say that God is redeeming all of creation, meaning not just the spiritual realm but the physical realm as well. Jayakumar Christian, a writer and the national director of World Vision India, said—and I'm paraphrasing him—"It's a travesty when we preach the gospel and it's drowned out by the rumblings of their stomach." There's a contradiction there; it doesn't make any sense to tell them about the God who loves them and cares about their every need when they're starving to death. It doesn't make any sense to do that.

RD: I love where you're going with this. I think the pendulum swings too far in one direction at times—like with soup kitchens where you have to listen to a gospel message before you get food. You don't preach the gospel to a drowning man, you throw him a life vest. But I know there are Christian organizations saying, "The pendulum has swung too far the other way. Now it's just about life vests, it's just about food."

MY: As Christians we're called to walk a delicate and extremely fragile balance between those two things. It's a razor's edge and you can fall off on either side. You can either be works focused or you can be word-focused, but we're supposed to love with both word and deed.

We all have had experiences with people for whom their agenda is more important than the actual conversation or than their listener. I never want to be someone who is coming into a conversation with an agenda. I want to be someone who is coming into a conversation with a true desire to know that person and to care for them as a creation of the God whom I love and serve. I don't need to convince them in twenty seconds that they need to follow Christ, but I need to love them and, insofar as it's appropriate, encourage them on the way toward Christ. That requires delicacy and a willingness to both shut up and to proclaim loudly. It's a kind of necessary malleability in the moment, I think.

The community house that Danae and I are living in right now—there are times when we need to say certain things to the men and women who live there, and there are times when we don't. We make no apology whatsoever about the fact that we are Christians and we are living in a Christian house and there are certain rules and responsibilities that come with that. But we also try to extend freedom to people to be where they are and to understand that coming to the Lord is a [process]. That being the case, we want to give them room to be able to say, "You know what, I don't want to talk about this right now." That's fine, I totally understand that you have space and you have grace and you have freedom to not talk about this right now—but know that we love you and that we are praying for you and that we want what's best for you.

I go back to this false dichotomy, this false idea that there's a spiritual realm and there's a physical realm, and as Christians we need to be only about the spiritual realm. The fact that Jesus came in the flesh—that God came as a human being—completely annihilates the separation we want to make between the physical and the spiritual. Jesus' incarnation brings the two together so that as Christians we have the responsibility and opportunity to be mindful of both. Jesus Himself was mindful both of people's spiritual state—proclaiming to them the coming kingdom of God—[and their physical state]—healing their diseases, feeding them when they were hungry, and being with them when they were lonely and in need and outcasts from society. That says to me that we need to put those two things together. It's all about living in both spheres.

ACKNOWLEDGMENTS

This book is the culmination of the efforts of many unnamed friends, supporters, and colleagues who have prayed, encouraged, reasoned, and questioned along the way. Of these, we especially thank Bridget Buckley (Christian's wife) for her vigorous dedication in securing interviews and background information. We also wish to thank Steve and Ann Buckley, Greg Hawkins, Dean Plumlee, and last but not least, Jason Myhre. Finally, we wish to thank each of the interviewees and their respective organizations, assistants, and staffs for helping us put this project together. To all the other unnamed: our sincerest gratitude.

NOTES

Introduction

1. John Calvin, *Truth For All Time*, 1536–1537, trans. Stuart Olyott (Edinburgh: Banner of Truth, 2008), 1–2.

2. *Webster's New World Dictionary*, Third College Edition.

3. *Nelson's New Illustrated Bible Dictionary* (Nashville: Nelson, 1995), 658. See also John 14:6.

4. Walter Rauschenbusch, *A Theology for the Social Gospel* (Nashville: Abingdon, 1987), 1.

5. A few suggestions for further reading would include Ron Sider's *Good News and Good Works*; *The Social Gospel, Religion and Reform in Changing America* by Ronald C. White and C. Howard Hopkins; and *A Theology for the Social Gospel* by Walter Rauschenbusch. For those more adventuresome, see Bono's speech to the National Prayer Breakfast and his interviews on the subject of Christian social investment.

Chapter 1: Is Doing Good, Good Enough?

1. Mark 10:46–52.

2. Charles Spurgeon, Sermon No. 1300, June 18, 1876, at the Metropolitan Tabernacle, Newington.

3. See *Strong's Dictionary*, entry G2784 *kēryssō*, and *Thayer's Lexicon*. The term is also used in describing what John the Baptist did in his ministry in Matthew 3:1 and Mark 1:4.

4. Walter Rauschenbusch, *Christianity and the Social Crisis* (New York: Harper & Row, 1964), 317.

5. Dietrich Bonhoeffer, "Jesus Christ and the Essence of Christianity," in *Dietrich Bonheoffer: Writings Selected* (Maryknoll, NY: Orbis Books, 2000), 45.

215

6. Ibid., 32.

7. Dietrich Bonhoeffer, *A Year with Dietrich Bonhoeffer*, ed. Carla Barnhill (New York: HarperOne, 2005), 225, quoting from *Ethics*.

Chapter 2: Socializing the Gospel

1. Martin Luther King Jr., *Stride Toward Freedom* (1958) in *The Social Gospel, Religion and Reform in Changing America*, Ronald White and C. Howard Hopkins (Philadelphia: Temple University Press, 1976), 274.

2. Available online at http://www.americanrhetoric.com/speeches/bononationalprayerbreakfast.htm.

3. Charles Sheldon, *In His Steps* (Chicago: Winston, 1937), 17–20.

4. Gerhard Uhlhorn, *Christian Charity in the Ancient Church* (Edinburgh: T and T Clark, 1883), 56–57.

5. White and Hopkins, *The Social Gospel*, xi, xvi, 255.

6. Walter Rauschenbusch, *Christianity and the Social Crisis* (New York: Harper & Row, 1964), xxi–xxii, 349.

7. C. Howard Hopkins, *The Rise of the Social Gospel in American Protestantism: 1865–1915* (New Haven: Yale University Press, 1967), 320.

8. Liam Goligher, *The Jesus Gospel: Recovering the Lost Message* (London: Authentic, 2006), 103–104, 132.

9. http://www.tonycampolo.org/sermons.php.

10. White and Hopkins, *The Social Gospel*, 279–80.

11. The Lausanne Covenant, Section 5, and The Lausanne Covenant: An Exposition and Commentary by John Stott, Copyright © 1975, Lausanne Committee for World Evangelization, available at http://www.lausanne.org/all-documents/lop-3.html.

12. Rauschenbusch, *Christianity and the Social Crisis*, 47.

13. Peter Singer, *The Life You Can Save* (New York: Random House, 2009), 19.

14. Taken from official White House Briefing Room release, Remarks of President Barack Obama, National Prayer Breakfast, February 5, 2009, Washington, DC.

15. Peter Singer, *The Life You Can Save*, xv.

16. Matthew 25:21.

Chapter 3: Three Truths

1. Even those theologians who maintain that eternal separation from God has some capacity for finality after which existence ceases would likely agree that such cessation occurs well into eternity.

2. C. S. Lewis, *The Great Divorce* (San Francisco: Harper Collins, 2001), ix.

3. See John 6:35–71; 7:37; 8:12, 31; 10:1–18.

4. John 11:25; 14:6.

5. Acts 2:38–41; 13:38–39; 17:30–31; 26:24–29; 28:23; 1 Peter 1:3–9; Romans 1:16–17; 5:6–11; Ephesians 2:1–10; 2 Corinthians 5:10, 14–21.

6. Acts 2:43; 2 Corinthians 12:12; and in general Acts 2, 9, 14, 20, and 28.

7. John 14:11; 20:30–31; Acts 2:22; Hebrews 2:4.

8. Matthew 4:23–25; 8–9; Luke 18 and 19 for these miracles.

9. Mark 10:46–52.

10. Matthew 5–7; 19:16–30; 22:37–40; Luke 10:25–37.

11. Mark 1:38; 4:35–36; 8:9–10; John 6:66.

12. Charles Spurgeon, *Morning and Evening* (Fearn, Scotland: Christian Focus, 1994), 342.

13. 2 Corinthians 4:7–5:10; Romans 8:18–23.

14. *Vines Complete Expository Dictionary* (Nashville: Thomas Nelson, 1996), 62, 86.

15. Matthew 18:29; Mark 1:40; 5:18, 23; 6:56; 7:32; 8:22.

16. Acts 8:4; Ephesians 4:11; 2 Timothy 4:5.

17. John 5:19–29; 6:35–40; 10:25–38; 12:44–45.

18. John 8:12; 9:39; 10:1–18; 11:25–26; 12:23–26; Matthew 16:24–28; Luke 18:18–23.

Chapter 4: Last-Breath Equality

1. R. C. Sproul, *Saved From What?* (Wheaton: Crossway Books, 2002), 45.

2. Matthew 16:21–28.

3. Matthew 4:1–17; Luke 2:49; 23:39–42; John 4:7–42.

4. Matthew 5:21–48; 6:19–21; 15:10–20.

5. Jean-Jacques Rousseau, *A Discourse on Inequality*, trans. Maurice Cranston (London: Penguin Books, 1984), 137.

6. Walter Rauschenbusch, *Christianity and the Social Crisis* (New York: Harper & Row, 1964), 213.

7. Ecclesiastes 1 and 2; 12:13.

8. Ecclesiastes 1:14; 12:13.

9. C. S. Lewis, *The Screwtape Letters* (San Francisco: Harper, 2001), 155.

10. Luke 16:19–31.

Chapter 5: Gospel-Rooted Humanitarianism

1. Matthew 26:11; Hebrews 9:27.

2. Isaiah 65:17; Romans 8:19–22; 2 Peter 3:10–13; Revelation 21:1–2.

3. John 5:30–43; 7:16–18, 28–29.

4. Romans 3:21–26; Ephesians 2:1–10; Colossians 1:15–22.

5. Luke 10:25–37; John 4:9.

Chapter 6: Go Forth and Conquer

1. John 6:66–68.

Interviews

1. From the sermon "On Freedom," delivered on July 24, 1932, in Berlin.

2. The 1981 Irish Hunger Strike was the culmination of a five-year protest during the "troubles" by Catholic Irish Republican prisoners in Northern Ireland that started in 1976. It was a showdown between the prisoners and the British government that generated massive global media interest. The strike was called off after ten prisoners starved to death.

3. Bob Pierce founded World Vision in 1950 and served until 1967. He founded Samaritan's Purse in 1970 and served until his death in 1978. Franklin Graham succeeded Pierce as president of Samaritan's Purse.

4. The Rwandan Genocide involved the 1994 mass killing of hundreds of thousands of Rwanda's Tutsi and Hutu political moderates over the course of approximately one hundred days.

5. Heraclitus [*floruit* (he flourished) 513 B.C.] in *Seven Against Thebes*, fragment 223.

6. See Proverbs 6:6.

WHEN HELPING HURTS

ISBN-13: 978-0-8024-5705-9

Churches and individual Christians typically have faulty assumptions about the causes of poverty, resulting in the use of strategies that do considerable harm to poor people and themselves. *When Helping Hurts* provides foundational concepts, clearly articulated general principles, and relevant applications. The result is an effective and holistic ministry to the poor, not a truncated gospel.

A situation is assessed for whether relief, rehabilitation, or development is the best response to a situation. Efforts are characterized by an "asset-based" approach rather than a "needs-based" approach. Short-term mission efforts are addressed, and microenterprise development (MED) is explored.

MOODY
PUBLISHERS
www.MoodyPublishers.com

INTO THE MUD

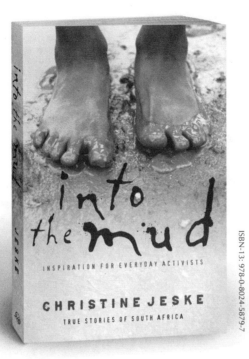

ISBN-13: 978-0-8024-5879-7

Into The Mud takes readers behind the headlines into real stories of real people living neck-deep in some of Africa's most difficult issues—but with hands, minds, and hearts rooted in God's kingdom. Each of its interwoven stories and related discussion questions address a broader issue of missions and development, including: evangelism, literacy and education, microfinance, health services, urbanization and refugee assistance, and more. Reflection questions at the end of each chapter help readers to apply lessons from the chapters to their own ministry contexts.

Where the world sees despair, author Christine Jeske sees God writing stories of hope. Study groups, development students, mission teams, and everyday activists alike will be challenged by her stories to enter more deeply into the thick of life's mud.

MOODY
PUBLISHERS

www.MoodyPublishers.com